A Taste of Creation

A Taste of Creation

Virginia Stem Owens

Judson Press ® Valley Forge

A Taste of Creation
Copyright © 1980
Judson Press, Valley Forge, PA 19481

All rights reserved. No part of this publication may be reproduced, stored in a retrieval system, or transmitted in any form or by any means, electronic, mechanical, photocopying, recording, or otherwise, without the prior permission of the copyright owner, except for brief quotations included in a review of the book.

Permission is gratefully acknowledged for use of the following articles from *Christianity Today:*

"Ripeness Is All," which was printed under the title "Go to the Garden Where Decay Redeems," December 17, 1976.
"The Price of Praise," November 18, 1977.
"The Separate Reality," which was printed under the title "Consider the Fingerprints of God," November 17, 1978.

Unless otherwise indicated, Bible quotations in this volume are from the Revised Standard Version of the Bible, copyrighted 1946, 1952, 1971, 1973 © by the Division of Christian Education of the National Council of the Churches of Christ in the United States of America, and are used by permission.

Other quotations of the Bible are from *The Holy Bible,* King James Version.

Library of Congress Cataloging in Publication Data
Owens, Virginia Stem.
   A taste of creation

   Includes bibliographical references.
   1. Meditations. 2. Owens, Virginia Stem.
I. Title.
BV4832.2.093   242   79-28076
ISBN 0-8170-0865-9

The name JUDSON PRESS is registered as a trademark in the U.S. Patent Office. Printed in the U.S.A.

PHOTO CREDITS: All photos in this book, except for the one on page 52, are by Virginia Stem Owens. The photo on page 52 is by Janice M. Gray.

*To my mother,
who taught me to name,
like Adam,
creation.*

Contents

The Price of Praise   9

The Cold Facts   17

The Terror and Treasure
    of the Snow   29

Light Hunger   39

Tasting the World   45

The Primal Metaphor   51

The Importance of Purple   57

The Pauline Prognosis   65

Anthood or Anarchy?   71

Mayflies in Gehenna   79

The Separate Reality   85

"Ripeness Is All"   93

Notes   101

The Price of Praise

I have a friend, an artist, who says the first thing she notices about a person is the colored splotch on the inner part of the eye socket where it curves upward to become a part of the nose, whether it is blue or purple or maybe slightly green. When she told me this, it startled me, and I was glad I was wearing glasses that hid my own little spot of color until I could go home and check it out for myself. If she had said that the first thing she noticed was the firmness of a person's handshake or the warmth of his smile or any of a dozen other characteristics by which we are admonished to judge people, I would not have felt self-conscious. But the inside of one's eye socket? That suddenly seemed a naked, vulnerable spot.

Charles Williams in *Descent of the Dove* says that people have sought God in two seemingly contradictory ways: through the senses (that is, by apprehending his creation) and through the suppression of the senses, what is called the *via negativa*. "The Way of Affirmation was to develop great art and romantic love and marriage and philosophy and social justice," he says; "the Way of Rejection was to break out continually in the profound mystical documents of the soul, the records of the great psychological masters of Christendom."

But the way of rejection is one that few have followed. Williams cites an ancient canon, dating from the second or third century, to illustrate the church's official attitude toward the material world: "If any bishop or priest or deacon, or any cleric whatsoever, shall refrain from marriage and from meat and from wine, *not for the sake of discipline but with contempt,* and, forgetful that all things are very good and that God made man male and female, blasphemously inveighs against the creation, let him be either corrected or deposed and turned out of the Church. And so with a layman" (italics mine).

Now in no way would I want to undermine the validity of the *via negativa*. It has had little enough honor, especially in the Protestant tradition, where deprivation of the senses is usually "for your own good" rather than for God's good. Indeed, how *any* good could derive from fasting, retreat, silence, or celibacy (despite our Lord's practice of them all) has often escaped our notice.

However, our defense of the former way, access to God through the full use of our senses, has of late been truncated and confused. The reasons are numerous and tiresome. For a start, most of the population is surrounded not by primary creation—the things that only God can make, such as trees—but by secondary or even tertiary creation, the things that God's creatures' creations can make, i.e., machines. And those secondary and tertiary products are often shoddy enough to merit only the cursory attention they get.

So that when my friend speaks of the subtle colors on human faces, it strikes us as extraordinary, a little odd, even faintly amusing, but not of the earthshaking importance it truly is. For how are we to give thanks for something we've never noticed? How shall we praise God for the world we've not paid proper attention to? Our practice of pigeonholing our praise into broad categories—family, friends, country, health, and the like—reminds me of the all-purpose, five-second prayer I devised as a child for use on cold nights: "God bless everybody in the world. Amen." When we pray in terms of everybody-in-the-world, we imagine ourselves to be dealing with a divine, omniscient bureaucracy. But God doesn't love everybody-in-the-world. He loves each of us singly, knowing the hairs of our heads and the shadows of our eye sockets.

One of the chief champions of this way of the senses in the Protestant tradition is, surprisingly, Jonathan Edwards, whose unfortunate reputation as a dour example of asceticism is due to his overly anthologized sermon "Sinners in the Hands of an Angry God." On the contrary, Edwards's early attention was absorbed by the natural sciences, the careful observation of spiders being his specialty. But natural science was not a mere sideline to his theological thought. His scrutiny of creation provided the full heart

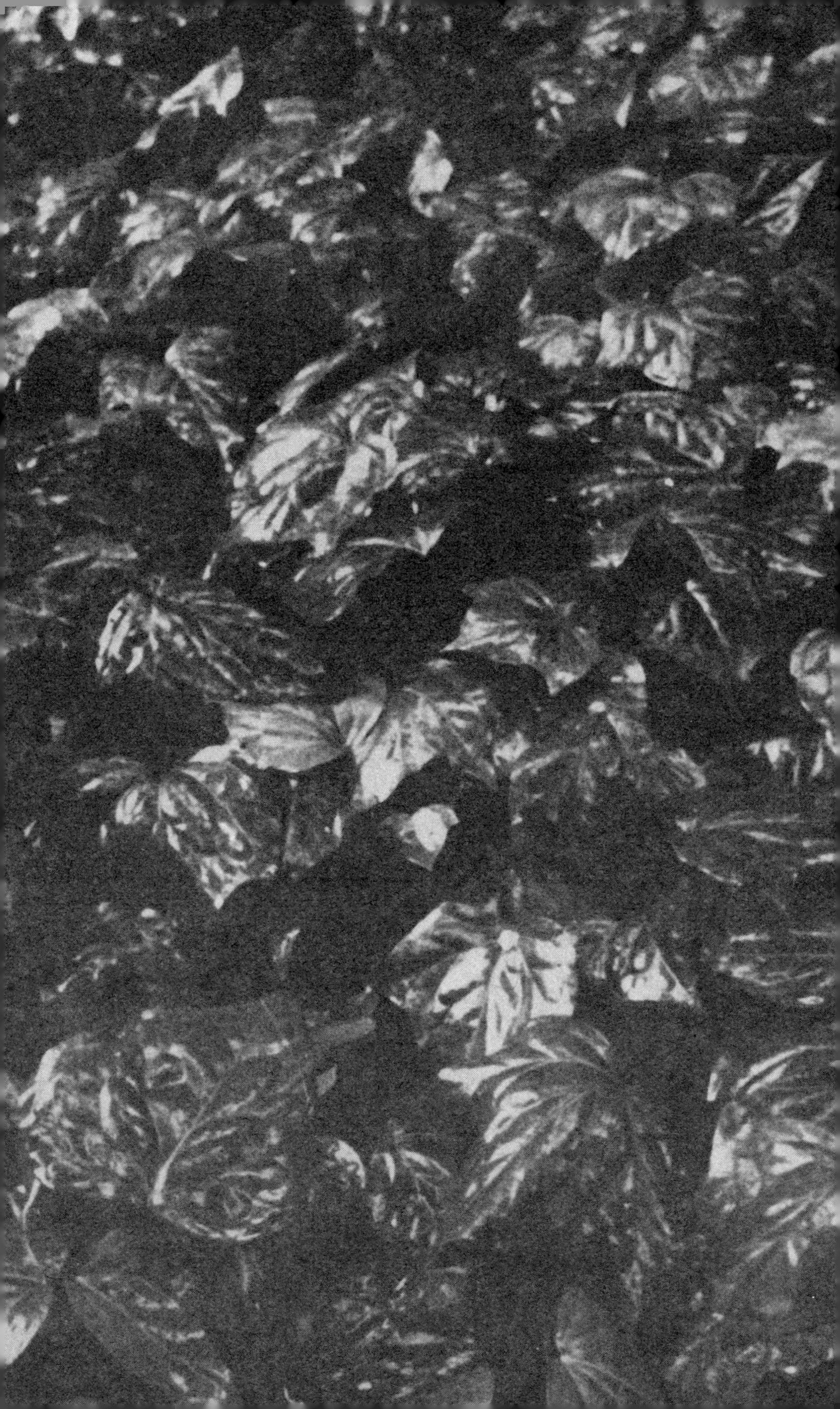

out of which he wrote his doctrine of creation, with which physics is only now catching up. ". . . God not only created all things, and gave them being at first, but continually . . . upholds them in being," he says. ". . . It will certainly follow from these things, that God's *preserving* created things in being is perfectly equivalent to a *continued creation,* or to his creating those things out of nothing *at each moment* of their existence."

Think of it. With each breath we take, God is again pumping into our lungs his exhalation of the breath of life, just as he did for Adam. If he withdrew his breath from the bubble of our world, we would instantly collapse. We are not clocks, once wound, running down. Developing this sense of continuous creation clears our hazy vision, enables us to see creation hanging on God's breath, dependent, contingent. And its precariousness makes it all the more precious.

The world's existence hangs on God's continuing to pay attention to it; to be properly thankful, we in turn must pay rapt attention to his crafting. But there are dangers. In *Pilgrim at Tinker Creek,* Annie Dillard tells of her meticulous search of her surroundings in rural Virginia, from the single-celled algae in her pond to the view of Alpha Centauri from her backyard. Sometimes the evidence in nature is devastating: nature is wasteful, extravagant, cruel, predatory. Never does the evidence point to chance, mere random agitation of atoms; and sometimes it points to the universe as the creation of a madman, a sadist. Yet it is beauty itself that is ultimately the answer to her questions, the fact that we desire and seek out beauty, that we separate the beautiful from the broken in creation. "No, I've gone through this a million times, beauty is not a hoax," she testifies. "Beauty is real. I would never deny it; the appalling thing is that I forget it." It takes attention, rapt attention, to keep that reality before us. But our attention span is limited. Is this not perhaps the meaning of sleep, that dark bed of mystery in which our consciousness must rest in order to be restored to its task of thanksgiving?

When Jesus instructed us to "consider" the lilies of the field and the fowls of the air, he wasn't making some moralistic point as in the dreadful fable of the ant and the grasshopper that was used to goad earlier generations into productive activity. The point of considering lilies is just the opposite: they are lazy lilies, occupying space amid the common field grasses for no reason other than that it pleases God. The idea of trillions of stars and cells offends our sense of proportion, especially as they keep exploding and dying. How can we praise such a wastrel, we who now are sweating out every barrel of oil and ton of coal? It's all very well for *him* to frivol about with wildflowers, but what about us—what shall we eat; what shall we drink; where shall we find fuel for the morrow?

Yet our business is not to be anxious about these matters but to praise God, to exult in him. And the most accessible way for most of us to do this is through God's creation. What we call nature—flowers and trees and birds and bees, scorpions and hail and sharks—is primary creation and reveals the "nature" of its Creator, the way he is. We know what steadfastness is because we see eons of predictability in the physical world. We know what surprise is because of sudden storms.

Andrew Wyeth once told an interviewer, "I love to study the many things that grow below the corn stalks and bring them back into the studio to study the color. If one could only catch that true color of nature—the very thought of it drives me mad." *That* is considering the lilies of the field. And it effectively shoulders aside utilitarian anxiety.

Or take for an example Rachel Peden, a woman of uncommon considering power, who in her book *Speak to the Earth* describes the exploration of a hound's-tongue seed: "The dime-sized seed pod is enclosed by five sepals and marked off into four parts with a single spike rising at the center. I pinched open one yellow-green, burry section of this fruitlet and saw the watery unripe seed inside. The brown stalk gave out an uninviting smell, sometimes compared to a mouse smell. . . . I liked it because it is pretty and interesting and we were having a good time fishing when I first saw hound's-tongue." On God's scale of knowledge which weighs heavier: knowing the market value of Nielsen ratings or knowing that a broken stalk of hound's-tongue smells mouselike?

Unfortunately, there is unrelenting pressure not to pay very close attention to creation but instead to consume oneself with anxiety about survival. A bizarre example of such pressure comes from a recent book called *Language and Woman's Place*. The author cautions women not to make fine color distinctions—not to speak of "mauve" and "lavender," for instance, because powerful people in our society lump them all together as "purple." (While Andrew Wyeth meticulously studies the various shades of snow.)

The demonic line of reasoning runs like this: If human senses, often employed to subvert the spirit, can also be a primary access to God in this world, then humanity must be harassed into not using them. "You see one mountain; you've seen them all," a friend, since demitted from the ministry, said to me. I felt the cold wind of blasphemy on my face. *Really seeing a mountain would take a lifetime,* I protested silently. Or longer than that if we are to believe Dante, who pictured purgatory as mountain shaped.

When Thornton Wilder wrote *Our Town,* his notion of purgatory was attention paid too late, misplaced in an afterlife of awareness devoid of action. When Emily dies in childbirth and joins the dead in the hillside cemetery, she longs to go back and observe just one day of her short life. The other inhabitants of the graveyard advise her to choose an ordinary, unimportant day because even the most mundane will prove overpoweringly poignant. Emily's final soliloquy echoes the lament of the psalmist who dreads to go down into the pit where there is no longer the possibility of praise. To the world that can no longer hear her Emily cries out her too-long-delayed passion for life and its ordinary splendors—the sound of clocks ticking, the brilliance of sunflowers, the smell and feel of freshly ironed clothes and steaming baths. She ends by asking the Stage Manager just how aware of life human beings really are as they are living it. His reply is not encouraging. It is only saints and poets who are awake enough to praise life, and then only sporadically.

My friend the artist, the observer of eye sockets, consented to give me drawing lessons. "It's simple eye-hand coordination," she insisted impatiently. Although I learned to excel in only two areas, long-haired sleeping dogs and aspen bark, I learned concomitantly to give thanks for a great many aspects of creation I had never known existed before. The great gaping holes in my universe were suddenly filled with such intricate detail that my eyes began to grow bulgy from looking. They felt too small to admit all the things there suddenly were to see: where the whiskers grow on a cat's nose and how exceptionally long they are, the receding ridges within a sandstone cave, the rounding slope of my daughter's upper lip.

"Divinity is not playful," Annie Dillard warns us. "The universe was not made in jest but in solemn incomprehensible earnest. By a power that is unfathomably secret, and holy, and fleet. There is nothing to be done about it, but ignore it, or see." Sometimes when I have been focusing overlong on the miniscule world of leafhoppers hatched in mold still damp from snowmelt, or when I feel physically assaulted by the bombardment of stimuli from a supposedly dead, silent winter day at my back door, I think it costs too much. The whole human race is not enough to search out each cunning device of its untiring creator. But attention is the price we must pay for awareness, without which there is no thanksgiving.

The Cold Facts

Winter is fierce in Wyoming. Even in the years when the snowfall is sparse and the temperature moderates above the mathematical zero, one watches the forecasts nervously, remembering that the great blizzard of 1949 was totally unpredicted. Howling in on the second day of the year, in a mere half hour it stranded holiday travelers on the long stretches of highway where one can drive for hours before reaching the next town. People froze in their cars during the four-day blow or were dug like rimed statuary out of drifts where they had stumbled searching for help.

Impatience was the worst enemy. Waiting out a storm is always the wisest plan. The insistence of our nerves that we do something, that we take up arms against the storm, assert ourselves, is almost always doomed. This past weekend, almost exactly thirty years after that blizzard, a man who was determined to bring help and left his two hunting companions in their stalled car, froze to death only one-half mile from where he set out. The ones who sat still survived.

During my first winter spent north of the thirty-eighth parallel, I would stand contemplating the accumulation of ice outside the glass doors of my Kansas apartment, the thought gradually forming itself in my mind: *A person could die out there.* The temperature of the air alone is sufficient to kill a human being.

Exposed flesh freezes at -31 degrees in sixty seconds. And if a twenty-five-mile-an-hour wind is blowing, flesh freezes at 14 degrees above zero. That is the kind of fact that frightens. My own southern flesh shudders at the implications. Despite the fact that ever since that

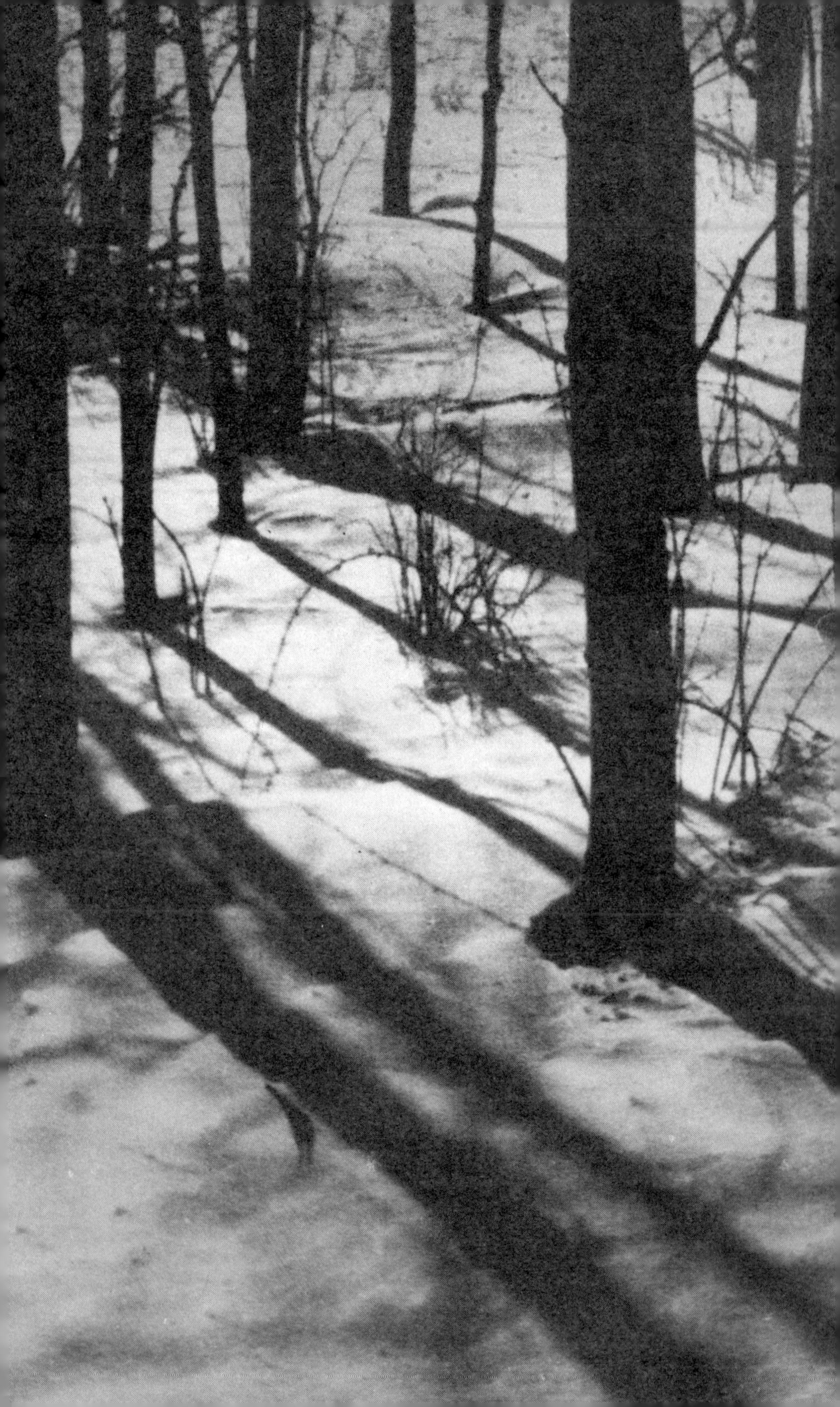

first Kansas storm I have never returned to tepid Texas winters, I am still affronted by weather that threatens human life. A little discomfort from a blustery day was the worst I knew of weather as a child, and I have not yet gotten over the shock of such rejection by a Mother whose Nature I had implicitly trusted. *You could die out there,* I keep whispering to myself in awe as I watch the wind whip the ice crystals horizontally through the air.

We once lived through a three-day blizzard in Colorado. It, too, was unpredicted and came up suddenly. We put blankets across the windows to keep out the penetrating cold. There was little light to let in anyway. I lay in bed for three nights, listening in fear to the enraged wind each time it lifted, waiting for the roof to be carried away, exposing us to the spiteful sky.

When the storm was over, people had died, some of them children, not many miles from our home. Cattle were frozen or suffocated with snow. Attics were full of drifts. Roofs had collapsed. Fences were down. Electricity was gone. Roads were closed. Even old-timers said it was the worst blizzard in living memory. A glacier that was sliding down the embankment behind our house all spring sheared off the new fruit trees buried beneath it as it ground southward.

It is all well and good claiming in a classroom that weather is neutral, that it has no predisposition, either kindly or cruel, toward us. But one only has to grow cold, then colder—the blood first flushing the skin in an attempt to warm the flesh, then, realizing danger, retreating strategically to the core of the body to try to keep at least the vital organs alive as the outer covering freezes and the cells crack open, diffusing their contents in what will never be flesh again—to feel that paranoid panic weather can bring on.

For weather is our whole atmosphere, our agar-agar in which we grow. Other hostile components of nature—rattlesnakes, scorpions, even bacteria and poison ivy—are localized enough so that we figure we can, with a certain amount of intelligent planning, outwit them. We can box them off and control them. But weather. It surrounds us, engulfs us, works its own will independently of our predictions. Meteorologists themselves admit that with the advent of all the new electronic and even extraterrestrial weather equipment, the reliability of their predictions has actually *decreased* over the past decade.

We sit on the surface of the earth like scuttling sea creatures on the ocean floor, caught in deep currents, watching the waves wash past the windows of our submerged sheltering shells. And winter is the worst of it. I watch the ice building up on the inside of aluminum storm sashes, and it is like the white fingers of the storm, probing into my safety from the outside, invading the small square of heated air that is all that protects what is human on this frozen plain.

Certain historians have credited cold weather with what we now call Western civilization. Certainly human civilization was born in the warm womb of the Fertile Crescent. Very possibly the unwieldy experiment might never have gotten off the ground had it not had this period of nurture in the earth's nursery. Why bands of humans should then have ever migrated northward over the fortieth parallel is still one of the essential mysteries of our history. Nomadic ventures across the Bering Straits from Siberia to the North American continent were made, not in a period of relative warmth but during the last Ice Age when land bridges were exposed by two hundred to three hundred feet of the world's water being captured in glacial sheets. Whatever it was that drove the race into the teeth of the storm is no doubt also responsible for what we know as technology today, that almost compulsive assertion of human dominance over Nature which is seen as enemy, not mother.

The Egyptians, working with the natural patterns of the Nile, simply waited for the floods to adjust their agriculture. The integrity of the Nile's nature, exasperating as it might be, was inviolable until the technology of the north asserted itself in the Aswan dam. Then the work of the Pharaohs, the monuments of stone built with the brawn of slaves rather than the clever devices of engineers, was drowned. The northern barbarians, their skills refined in a furnace of ice, had returned in a kind of Freudianism of historic dimensions to conquer the nourishing mother we call Nature. Now the entire Middle East, where the human story began, is nailed down with oil derricks, hypodermics that suck sustenance from beneath the skin of the earth. It is from Florida that rockets repel the pull of Mother Earth to nose the unknown with outrageous arrogance, but the technology belongs to a colder climate. It was in the extreme latitudes of the northern hemisphere that humanity learned that Nature was an improvident parent to be outwitted rather than trusted. It was there that the notion of a harmonious filial relationship with the environment died a bitter death. We must not be too sanguine in our hopes for a reconciliation.

I once thought it strange that the mountain states in this country were the strongest bastion against the environmentalist cause. To the rest of the country these areas are the apotheosis of natural beauty, the subject of calendar art and the object of flatlanders' fantasy. Rushing mountain streams, alpine meadows full of flowers, forests of mystery and majesty. "America the Beautiful," our national hymn to beauty, was, after all, written from the top of Pike's Peak. Yet the inhabitants of these states, particularly the farmers and ranchers, have an exceptionally hard place in their hearts for Nature. She is first of all their formidable foe. A killer who slaughters more wantonly than a wolf pack. A mean-spirited miser who, at her most magnanimous, sends adequate amounts of water in the form of snowmelt to supply one season's irrigation. I have learned not to expect sentiment over the drying marshlands of migrating whooping cranes in Nebraska when a dam is planned in Wyoming to harbor the pitifully moisture-poor snow produced in subzero weather.

The stony faces of the wheat growers are not mobile with emotion like those of the bird defenders. They have frozen in too many Wyoming winters. It is not that they do not care about whooping cranes. But they see the birds as hostages, balanced against agriculture by their enemy, Nature, with whom the farmers are engaged in a lifelong battle. It is just one more skirmish that makes winning the war harder. In fact, they never actually expect to win. They know the overwhelming power they are pitted against. There are no Walt Whitmans among them, supinely contemplating the leaves of grass. The talk of harmony with Nature is to them quisling propaganda, advocating collaboration with the enemy. Try harmonizing your 98.6-degree body temperature with a -90-degree windchill factor.

Why don't they leave, then? Why do they continue to bear the incredible physical stress and the extremities of economic contingency? For answer there is only a silent shrug. They themselves don't know. They are in the combat zone with Nature, and somehow they can't justify retreating behind the lines. Their warfare has defined them. Take away their enemy, and their hard-edge contours would dissolve like a fine filigree of frost melting in the sun.

Winter in the United States and Canada occasions some of the world's most extreme weather, first of all because the northern hemisphere, in general, is stormier than its southern counterpart. But the continental land mass of North America has only mountain ranges running roughly north and south. The great east-west humps of the Alps and the Himalayas moderate the effects of swirling polar air for the continents of Europe and Asia. But the Appalachians and, more importantly, the Rockies act as funnels to direct the flow of frigid air down across the unobstructed face of America.

There is nothing very temperate about our temperate zone. Nine-tenths of our continent experiences wild fluctuations in temperature during winter. In the monster winter of 1949 when temperatures in Wyoming and Montana were falling twenty-five to thirty degrees below the mean from normal (which is in itself extreme), the eastern tier of states were having twelve to nine degrees *above* their normal mean. San Diego had its first recorded snowfall, while Washington, D.C., had a record high of seventy-three degrees. It is not uncommon for weather stations on the eastern face of the cordillera to find the thermometer falling sixty degrees in a twenty-four-hour period.

Is it a racial strain of masochism that accounts for Wyoming ranchers and polar explorers like Admiral Byrd? He spent four and one-half months alone on the Ross Ice Shelf, a web of water frozen to a depth of seven hundred feet between the toes of the continent of Antarctica. Cut off by 150 miles from the main expedition at Little America where they had, through some strange outworking of ingenuity, even managed to sequester underground three cows in the polar night, he was still hundreds of miles from the pole. The meteorological information he was able to record at Advance Camp was not so greatly different from that at Little America as to merit the incredible suffering he endured there.

In his personal account of that quite literal dark night of the soul, he feels constrained to return over and over to his motivations for seeking out this razor-thin edge of survival. Often the reasons jostle one another in their claims. He coveted time for reflection, he says, to sort out a philosophy from the warehouse of his explorer's brain, clogged and haphazardly crammed with details and worries of being the expedition leader and organizer. There are, of course, other simpler and safer ways of attaining solitude if that is one's true desire. But perhaps he knew his own limitations; he knew it would have to be a solitude enforced by such a rigorous necessity as only the Antarctic winter could assure. It was outside of human power to reach him once the sun began to set on his buried shelter shack on the Barrier.

This is a configuration of circumstances totally different from those surrounding Thoreau's retreat to Walden Pond. Winter for him was a lazy lull, a pleasant change in the time signature of the year's music. He watched the squirrels, the foxes, the jays, and the owls; he stoked his fire cheerfully; he entertained the New England illuminati and lectured weekly in Concord, walking through the sea of snow, dry shod on a carpet of dark oak leaves that absorbed the sun's heat and melted the ice away.

Perhaps it was because Thoreau had already been to Walden Pond that Richard Byrd had to go to Antarctica. Perhaps life can never, for once and all, be "driven into a corner" as Thoreau proposed to do, but must be repeatedly pushed to its limits. Perhaps what he called "the essential facts of life" must be tested for accuracy over and over again, as though one had to try individually each molecule of oxygen for its specific gravity. Both men wanted to end the uncertainty of life "whether it is of the devil or of God"; yet the answer, secured at whatever cost, seems ultimately untransmissable. It is as though the Virginian had said to the New Englander, "It's all very well and good, your holing up in a cozy hut with friends dropping in from time to time. You became awfully chummy with Nature. But did you drive her far enough into a corner? Is there not a point when she will turn on you and rip open the skin of your self-deceiving satisfaction? What, after all, *are* the limits?" Still, their line of questioning is in the same direction. It is only the degree that differs. Thoreau's was at 42°30′ north, while Byrd's was at 80°08′ south.

"It's not getting to the pole that counts," wrote Byrd. "It's what you learn of scientific value on the way. Plus the fact that you get there and back without being killed." To Thoreau, science was a matter of amusement. Certainly he never tired of parenthetically inserting the proper Latin names for the Massachusetts flora and fauna, much as one embroiders useful household objects. And he went to great and careful lengths to map the bottom of frozen Walden

Pond. But a southerly breeze had blown the softening influence of the Vedas into his soul. The idea of either science or survival as a value would have been laughable to Thoreau. Yankee mirth growing out of eastern mysticism. A bit too easy for Byrd.

"That must be a poor country indeed that does not support a hare," blithely wrote Thoreau from the protection of the temperate zone. *Precisely,* thought Byrd. And thus to such a poor country he betook himself, one that supports not even its native penguins during its long black night. He admits that "perhaps, the desire was also in my mind to try a more rigorous existence than any I had known." (Remember that he had already been to the North Pole and had flown over the South Pole.) "Where I was going, I should be physically and spiritually on my own. Where Advance Base was finally planted, conditions were not very different from what they were when the first men came groping out of the last Ice Age."

Ice. Both in image and in fact, it frightens our warm blood worse than any other aspect of our environment. We may burn with anger, but terror is always cold. It is chills we get up and down our spines at the thought of our extinction. Cold-blooded murder we judge worse than a crime of passion. Fire at least brings light, but it is the darkness that pulls the cold over us. The drift of our whole human heritage is shadowed by our preference for warmth in our metaphors. A cold heart or feet or stare—of none of these do we approve. Having lived most of my life in lands that sustained some of the earth's hottest temperatures, I know now that however miserable and lethargic one grows there, life is still possible, indeed often proliferates in such climates. India, where the temperature reaches 120 degrees, teems with human bodies, however malnourished, whereas Antarctica is so inhospitable to human habitation that its population shifts yearly and it remains the one land mass no country will fight for. Its only political identity is an international treaty that protects scientific investigation. Yet it doubles its square footage once every year simply by freezing its borders. During that polar night it captures 90 percent of the world's fresh water.

This is ice: not a palace but a prison. It locks up the elements most necessary for life. At least four times in the past billion years it has covered the globe like an eggshell. Eighteen millennia ago the glacial sheet began its latest diminution. It took it twelve thousand years to uncover Canada's top side. That great land mass, released from the weight of the ice as from a winter overcoat, is still bouncing back, lifting its continental shoulders as much as eight inches annually.

Human civilization as we know it, that fragile and altogether unique creation, is only ten thousand years old. Its timing was, in retrospect, perfect. The optimum temperature since the glaciers last began their sullen retreat came about eight thousand years ago. The world was even warmer then than it is now. Summertime in ancient Sumer, and the living was easy—all the way from the Nile Valley to the Persian Gulf. Several fluctuations—minor by the macrocosmic standards in which a millennium is the unit of measurement—have occurred since then. Before the time of Moses, eight hundred years of drought that turned the once-lush Arabian peninsula into a desert through which the Israelites would wander were followed by a cooler, wetter period during which the Medes invaded Assyria and the Dorians swept into Greece. The next warm, dry millennium saw the golden ages of Greece and Rome, but the resulting droughts saw the failing of the forests of Lebanon and the roses of Sharon. The next cold, wet cycle brought the northern barbarian hordes down upon Rome. And the succeeding thaw between A.D. 800 and 1000 allowed the great Viking voyages of discovery and the colonization of Greenland which produced lavish crops.

It was a brief respite in the world's weather, however. By A.D. 1200 it was ice, not crops, that grew in Greenland. The Baltic Sea froze solid in 1422-23. The last Greenlander had starved by the end of the century. The long winter of what is called the Little Ice Age was more tenacious. Look at the paintings done north of latitude 40º during this period, and notice the astonishing amount of clothes that covered the human body so dear, undraped, to the artist's eye. All the figures in Greek and Roman art had been in langorous dishabille. Now they are bundled up to their necks in fur-trimmed cloaks and hats. Only in an attitude of suffering are they stripped.

The invasion and settlement of the North American continent took place during this Little Ice Age. When we call the Puritans a cold and frigid people, perhaps we should remember this extenuating circumstance. Much of the pathos of the American Revolution—the bloody footprints at Valley Forge, the guns dragged across the frozen river to Staten Island—is owing to the world's being sunk in what must have seemed an interminable winter which didn't break for the northern temperate zone till the middle of the last century. Indeed, the last one hundred years have been the mildest since that warm period when civilization first began. World population has doubled in this benign period. Canadians grow wheat one hundred miles further north.

But can we trust the world to remain hospitable? In the last decade the world's temperature has begun to fall off sharply again, according to the U.S. National Science Board. For much of the past billion years the average global temperature has been around an ideal seventy-two degrees. Today it hovers at fifty-eight degrees. The ice shell on Greenland, where breadfruit trees once grew, and on Antarctica, is two miles thick. We fumble with the facts, trying to establish where we are in relation to a predicated cosmic pulse that seems to indicate beats of 250 million years with closer fluctuations every hundred thousand years and between that—what? And what can time periods that vast mean to human beings whose three score and ten can scarcely even be located on such a chart?

We measure distance to the stars in parsecs, abstractions of space that defeat us in their enormity. It is the same with time. How early I dare to set out my tomato plants this spring and whether they will have time to ripen in September are the questions that concern me. I can't be bothered with the next Ice Age except as it affects my garden. Even the scientists for whom sunspots and deep-sea currents and Antarctic ice cores are raw materials where they dig and delve as I turn over the topsoil in my garden—even they cannot formulate more than a theoretical worry for weather past the generation of their grandchildren. *Why worry,* we mutter to ourselves like Hezekiah did when Isaiah prophesied the Babylonian captivity for his descendants, *why worry if there will be peace and security in my days?* The human spirit simply cannot support its concern for posterity past two generations. "I'll be dead by then anyway"; we comfort ourselves with that grisly certainty.

Ice is a much more certain enemy than nuclear destruction, but our great-grandchildren are on their own, out in the cold.

The heart has limits just as surely as the flesh does. If Hezekiah's attitude offends us, let it, along with the weather, also humble us.

Despite our pretensions to peace and goodwill, we are not capable of caring into the next Ice Age. It will take all our wisdom just to warm ourselves. Even the legacy we leave our grandchildren is likely to be no more than a pittance. If there is a fire that burns for future families of humankind, it must be some steadier, surer source of heat than our sun or ourselves.

The Terror and Treasure of the Snow

A cold wind is all it takes to make me as apolitical as Thoreau. Weather has always been the major yet unacknowledged partner in every power shift in human history. Hadrian and Napoleon failed in their campaigns not from inferior intelligence or moral turpitude; they were defeated by snow, that white eraser that moves relentlessly across the page of history and leaves it blank again. There is a certain amount of Thoreauvian ironic pleasure I take in laughing up my long flannel sleeves at the furrowed and sweating brows of politicians whose schemes and philosophies are unwittingly based on the blithe assumption that the Florida Keys will never see frost nor Siberia become the Sahara. The circumpolar vortex slipping its southern scallops only a few hundred miles eastward could undo the entire globe's political structures during one president's tenure with no reference to his party preference.

Oil—fossil fuel—is currently the political fact that overrides every social theory devised by humans. It is the balmy weather of more than a million years ago that has made the Arab nations suddenly rich and powerful. We suck the dinosaur deposits from under the Arctic ice and the desert floor, neither of which can now support the meagerest agriculture. Jesus rebuked the power seekers of his day for being able to discern the face of the sky but not the signs of the time. We pride ourselves on our dubious analysis of social, moral, and economic trends today, but, having been desensitized to weather by central heat and air conditioning, we cannot read the skies. We need a weather eye more than universal suffrage perhaps.

We have forgotten our precarious place on this planet, lulled in a few short millenia into cozy security. Yet Greenland once plummeted from a plateau of comparative comfort into the implacable abyss of an ice age in less than one hundred years.

On the other hand, our technological weather eye has opened so wide that we do not even know how to assimilate all the information it is capable of taking in. Sunspots, ice caps, volcanic eruptions, magnetized deep-sea currents, continental drift, blinks of solar radiation, wobbles in the earth's own axis. Ancient agriculturalists knew nothing of these, yet their accuracy in predicting a humanized scale of weather—meaning whether or not to plant barley—was probably better than our own.

We are the victims of too much data. And of time. We can only play with our technology like a child with a toy toolbox. The National Oceanic and Atmospheric Administration's computer at Princeton is one of the fastest in the world; still, it takes six hours of feeding it facts before it can regurgitate a calculation of global weather for one day. And one missing bit of data, one unforeseen phenomenon, can make the whole effort a vain striving. The incalculable wild cards that have only recently entered the game—particulate matter flung up into the atmosphere by an exploding population doing no more than shuffling its feet, much less plowing, driving, manufacturing, and trying to keep warm around some form of combustible material—all these cannot even be chopped up fast enough to be fed to the fact eater. We literally know too much for our own good. Facts that we cannot string together in any coherent fashion on the chain of cause and effect simply fall from our information storage closets in a jumble of unsorted systems.

And allied against us with the cold is our even more ancient enemy Time. The two make a cunning pair. It is painful to remember that we speak of being "frozen in time." Time, like terror, is always cold.

The single most constant factor in this conundrum of the world's weather is the sun, the fulcrum of our planetary clock. Any hope of heat we know comes from that source. The solar constant—that is the comforting name we have given this flood of life-giving light that bathes our orb. O wise Parsees! To lift your eyes above the auxiliary organizations of mundane deities and fix your gaze on the ball of fire

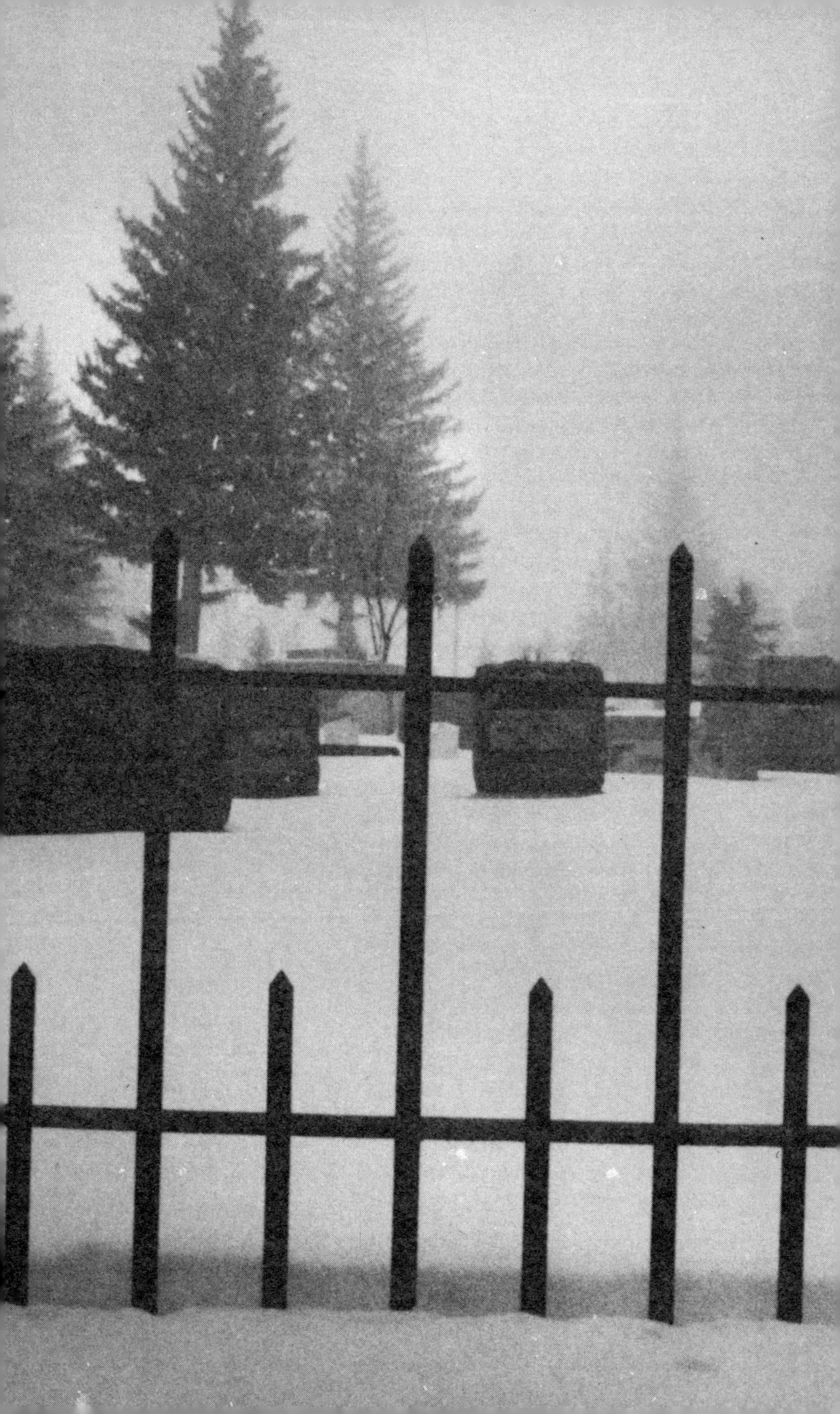

that fuels our planetary destiny. Without benefit of computer or satellite you realized the sun was the source.

But how boundless the despair of the modern pagan who knows, as the trusting Parsees did not, that the fuel is, after all, finite! Not in our lifetime though, say the modern Hezekiahs. That lazy old sun will keep on rolling round heaven for more days than will mean anything to us.

Perhaps. But there is also concern among the theorists that (unspeakable thought) the sun flickers like a dysrhythmic heart. Oh, maybe not more than once in a million or even a billion years. But this is the kind of unsubstantiatable fact that drives scientists mad. A row of scientists strung end-to-end through all of human history would not be enough to observe one fluctuation from the core of our solar system. No instrument for monitoring the solar constant was included on the manned moon shots of the 1960s. The project was abandoned for the reason that keeping such a delicate piece of machinery operating and accurately calibrated even over the short space of a century was unfeasible. A blink in the sun is a ponderous thing; it does not occur in the wink of an eye as with our hearth fires. The continents rebound in excruciatingly slow motion from shedding their ice coats. Who can say how long it would take the sun to blink its burning eye?

Going up? The elevator operator on the world's thermometer leers at us knowingly. We stutter with indecision. One scientific contingent thinks so; another objects that all the signs point down. And a third simply shrugs. The effects of our recent activity on the planet make it impossible to tell. We may be living in either an incipient greenhouse or a refrigerator. Only Time will tell. We stumble aboard the elevator and Time shuts the door, grinning. We really have no choice anyway. He pushes the button, but we cannot discern whether we're ascending to warmth or dropping into polar regions.

One thing is sure, however. More cold is death to creatures such as we are. And already we are fourteen degrees below the Climatic Optimum that ended four thousand years ago. Every molecule of water that the ghostly Ice King turns to stone means that much less life on this unpredictable planet. As he set up his solitary site in the Antarctic, Byrd despaired at all the "countless things required to defend existence in a place which offers nothing to man but air to breathe." I underscore the words to point out how the most scientific mind cannot avoid the metaphoric implications of our enmity with ice.

Let us slip into the territory of the enemy, however; "the treasures of the snow" is a godly taunt thrown up to Job in his theodicy. And we find terror and beauty locked in an undeniable, incomprehensible embrace. Yet are not all our enemies ugly and squalid? What is hostile to human life—must not its moral repugnance be mirrored in its outward manifestation? Not here. Its austere beauty is not a deception like that of Snow White's wicked stepmother. The beauty of the Snow Queen is unapproachable yet genuine.

Crystal was the ancient Greeks' word for ice. They had the notion that mineral quartz was no more than permanently hardened water, ice that never melted. But it was Olaus Magnus, archbishop of Upsala, who attempted the first study of snow crystals in 1555. The exceptionally clumsy woodcuts used as illustrations, however, proved to be an unacceptable medium for the delicacy of the subject. It was not until 1820 that snow crystals, a more ancient phenomenon than humankind itself, were copied with any degree of painstaking accuracy and this by the Arctic explorer William Scoresby who was torn between the economic necessity of whaling and the fascination of observation. A few years later in 1832, Toshitsura Doi, a feudal lord in Japan, brought out *Sekka Zusetsu,* or *Illustration of Snow Blossoms.* The interior structure that showed itself in the surprising symmetry of snow crystals had finally succeeded in catching the eye of man.

Perhaps the greatest proof of this pervasive fascination lies in the life of Wilson A. Bentley. He was not a scientist or even a feudal lord with time and talent on his hands. He was a Vermont farmer who happened to have been given a microscope for his fifteenth birthday. Since that fell in February, it also happened that what presented itself as a likely subject for amateur microscopy was a skyful of ice stars.

They became a lifelong obsession. Bentley never married. His heart had been glamoured by the Snow Queen. He inhabited only three rooms of the family homestead and an icy shed where he had his snowflake equipment. Since he had none of Toshitsura Doi's artistic abilities, he had to rig an incredibly complicated system for making photomicrographs of the crystals. First he had to catch the snow crystal on a smooth black board, hurry into the shed before the catch was blown away, inspect it with a magnifying glass for photogenic suitability, and then transfer it to a glass microscope plate where it was gently stroked into position by a small wing feather. A camera (such as they were in the 1880s) was attached to the microscope; both were focused separately, pointed toward the sky, and exposed for twenty long seconds.

He collected nearly six thousand photomicrographs of snow crystals this way over a forty-year period, dying finally of pneumonia on Christmas Eve. Yet for all his painstaking, Bentley was not a scientist. His selection of crystals was sheerly on aesthetic grounds. Almost offhandedly he learned something of the connections between meteorological conditions and the shapes they are likely to produce. But the study of molecular crystallography did not interest him. It was the beauty of miniature intricacy that fueled his passion.

Scientists—German, Japanese, Norwegian—pressed on, however, and inward toward the secret of the snow crystal. They learned that vapor, crystallizing in a free, supercooled atmosphere, achieves seemingly endless variations within the rigid confines of the hexagon. A snow crystal is now the symbol of the universal artistic tension: improvisation within the immutable boundaries of form. The proverbial "no two snowflakes alike" has been expanded by observation. Actually, *the two sides of a single snow crystal* most often differ in detail. Yet the basic structure cannot vary. They are all, from the smallest "diamond dust" crystal, 8/1000 of an inch in diameter, that forms just above the ground out of a fog bank, to the large wet spring snowflakes up to 3/16 of an inch, bound to the unshakable structure of the water molecule: two hydrogen atoms, positively charged, circling an oxygen atom, negatively charged, with 120-degree angles separating the hydrogen atoms from each other and from the negative charge of the central oxygen atom. These molecules must interlock in a way that builds on a complex weave of threes and sixes to produce an infallible electromagnetic tissue of ice called the "crystal lattice." It takes sixty water molecules to make the simplest ice crystal, too small to see. The average snowflake on the sidewalk contains 100 million or more molecules. Snowflakes do not "do their own thing"; they adhere to the classic rules of crystals. Compared to this, the structure of a sonnet is a loose and easy yoke. Yet they are the very symbol of diversity.

Some snowflakes are indeed stars or dendrites, as scientists call them. Others are hexagonal plates; some are hollow six-sided columns, capped either by larger plates or hexagonal needle noses. Yet even the asymmetrical crystals, broken by storm and wind and tossed together like snowflake salad, still must abide by the inexorable law of positive and negative attraction and the unbending 120-degree angle.

There are minds, and perhaps they are the true but unrecognized guardians of aesthetics in this century, to whom the arrangement of molecules, their density, falling velocity, and electrical charges are the occasions for ecstasy. Ravished by such pure intellectual beauty, they cannot know enough, cannot penetrate too far the privacy of such profligate trifles piling up by the trillions in the street. Yet the one mystery that eludes them is the reason why there should be such infinite variations on a single, relatively simple, six-sided theme.

And that is only the visual part of this beauty. Helen Keller, blind and deaf, found herself in the midst of a ferocious blizzard in Cleveland in the winter of 1913. The winds reached seventy-nine miles an hour, and after two days the city was left under a twenty-one-inch blanket of snow. She could neither see the snow nor hear the screaming wind; yet she experienced the storm of invisible electrical charges that bombarded the earth. She recounts:

> "I knew it was storming before I was told. The rooms, the corridors, everywhere within the building vibrated with the power of the storm without—when I knew it was snowing as it never had in this part of the world, I wished to rush out and throw myself into the snow and ride upon the tempest. . . . I am stirred to the depth of my being by the storm, and my body, mind and soul are better for this great experience—the greatest of its kind in my life. Few times in my life has it been given me to feel sensations akin to those I have experienced as a captive of the blizzard. . . ."

Perhaps it takes the extraordinary configuration of events that make up the life of Helen Keller to reveal to the rest of us, prisoners of our own sight and hearing, the fuller dimension of storm, the minute tactile vibrations, the electrical stimulation that drew her, literally like a magnet, that tempted her "to ride upon the tempest." She, seemingly the most vulnerable of humans, yearned for union with an aspect of Beauty we can scarcely apprehend.

Admiral Byrd, isolated in Antarctica, the single spectator to the sensuous yet austere delights of the aurora australis, felt himself transformed by this cosmic light show.

> The day was dying, the night being born—but with great peace. Here were the imponderable processes and forces of the cosmos, harmonious and soundless. Harmony, that was it! . . . In that instant I could feel no doubt of man's oneness with the universe. The conviction came that that rhythm was too orderly, too harmonious, too perfect to be the product of blind chance—that, therefore, there must be purpose in the whole and that man was a part of that whole and not an accidental offshoot. It was a feeling that transcended reason; that went to the heart of man's despair and found it groundless. The universe was a cosmos, not a chaos. . . .

Brave words, Admiral Byrd. And true enough, no doubt, for that moment. But it was not many days before Terror rose up to dance with Beauty before you, and the question of "man's oneness with the universe" was once again raised.

Having lost himself on the Barrier through absorption in an overextended interior monologue, Byrd finds the aurora going on with the show with apparent unconcern for his situation. The glorious streamers and curtains of light continue their dance in the polar night while panic freezes his heart. He manages to make his way back to his hut at last where he reconsiders: "Yet, this harmony was mostly of the mind: a temporary peace won by a physically occupied body. But the glory of the celestial is one, and the glory of the terrestrial is another. Even in my most exalted moods I never quite lost the feeling of being poised over an undermined footing, like a man negotiating a precipice who pauses to admire the sunset, but takes care where he places his feet."

Where is this "oneness with the universe" now? The harmony in which we suppose ourselves to be the tonic chord—our ears strain after it but hear instead the creak of ice as the crevasse opens before us. Is this world, even this spinning blue ball, friendly to humankind? No one of unclouded sensibilities discredits the harmony certainly. A single snowflake is enough to dispel our fear of chaos. But if all human flesh condensed into chemicals, would the harmony be less?

Would not the world turn, the snowflakes fall, with aloof equanimity? Unlike the rest of the natural world, we do not even provide food for the ecological balance. No species is so extraneous. How do we dare to talk of harmony and oneness when winter shoulders us aside, forces us apart into artificial environments? Do we not, indeed, merely hang around the edges of the cosmos, able to see only a narrow band of light, to hear a thin range of sound waves, to survive a small scale of temperature?

It is this that Jehovah reminds Job of when he answers him out of the whirlwind: that the universe was not created for his particular amusement. To presume to be one with the universe is a buffoon's idea of a joke.

> "From whose womb did the ice come forth,
> and who has given birth to the hoarfrost of heaven?
> The waters become hard like stone,
> and the face of the deep is frozen."

It seems the Almighty makes the rain to fall not simply on the just and the unjust but also in the waste places where there are no human habitations at all. And if the world is full of creatures not always bright and beautiful but sometimes fearsome and predatory, the creations that are Leviathan and Behemoth do not depend in any way on our approval for their continued existence.

When Ransom, C. S. Lewis's hero of the space trilogy, discovers the underworld of the planet Perelandra, he realizes in humility that "the inside of this world is not for man." The mute exotic form he encounters there "was no doubt his fellow creature. It did not follow that they were equals or had an equal right in the under-land."

Solitary on the ice cap, Admiral Byrd finally concludes something similar: "I watched the sky a long time, concluding that such beauty was reserved for distant, dangerous places, and that nature has good reason for exacting her own special sacrifices from those determined to witness them."

The glory of God is not all sweetness and light. It is also darkness and cold. Our aesthetic sensitivities to this fact are blunted by our prior need for sheer survival. Our own predilection for existence cannot help but temper our enthusiasm for Beauty encased in Terror. It was all very well for Admiral Byrd to speak of his oneness with the universe until he nearly literally accomplished that goal by falling into a crevasse several hundred feet deep. It was then that he drew back from the icy embrace of the universe, terrified by that promise of unity with inhuman creation.

No. If it is union our spirits seek, it had better be sought for elsewhere, at the source of creation. Not all things were created in his image, and the faces they show to mortals, though beautiful, can freeze our hearts with their cold and alien cruelty. God demands of Job:

> "The wings of the ostrich wave proudly;
> but are they the pinions and plumage of love?"

The winter winds do not whistle with the Word that is love, but they are a scourge to drive us from an untimely wedding with the universe.

Light Hunger

This is the second day we have felt, like Lazarus, the graveclothes loosening. It would be too much to say one could actually feel spring in the air, but we could tell that winter would not last forever, that death and dark and cold were not the end.

The first day I knew this was yesterday at the V.A. hospital. Although I was indoors, hurrying along corridors that reeked with the pent-up flatus of winter from wards where no window had opened for months, I could see the sun, stronger and slanting at a peculiar angle onto the snow that turned the earth around its edges dark with melt. The smell of this sarcophagus, a great gullet down which slides the sloughings-off of human flesh, was then more repugnant than ever, and I knew by the very violence of my recoil from this unventilated cave of disease and death that life was asserting itself again with the light.

All winter long we have gone about resigned to the lessening of the light and life. The days in the grave are inevitable. The solstice itself did little to relieve the outlook. The sun does not, after all, following the third week in December, burst back upon the horizon, bringing an early and easy jubilation to the planet. Lazarus lingered in the tomb four days. The scent of death was strong. And we, in our winter night, have stumbled along, our faith in the light's return lessening with each bleak day. Wolf-madness, we learn from Robert Burton's *Anatomy of Melancholy,* is always worst in February when it inhabits graveyards and barren fields.

The part of us that reads books, that devises calendars and

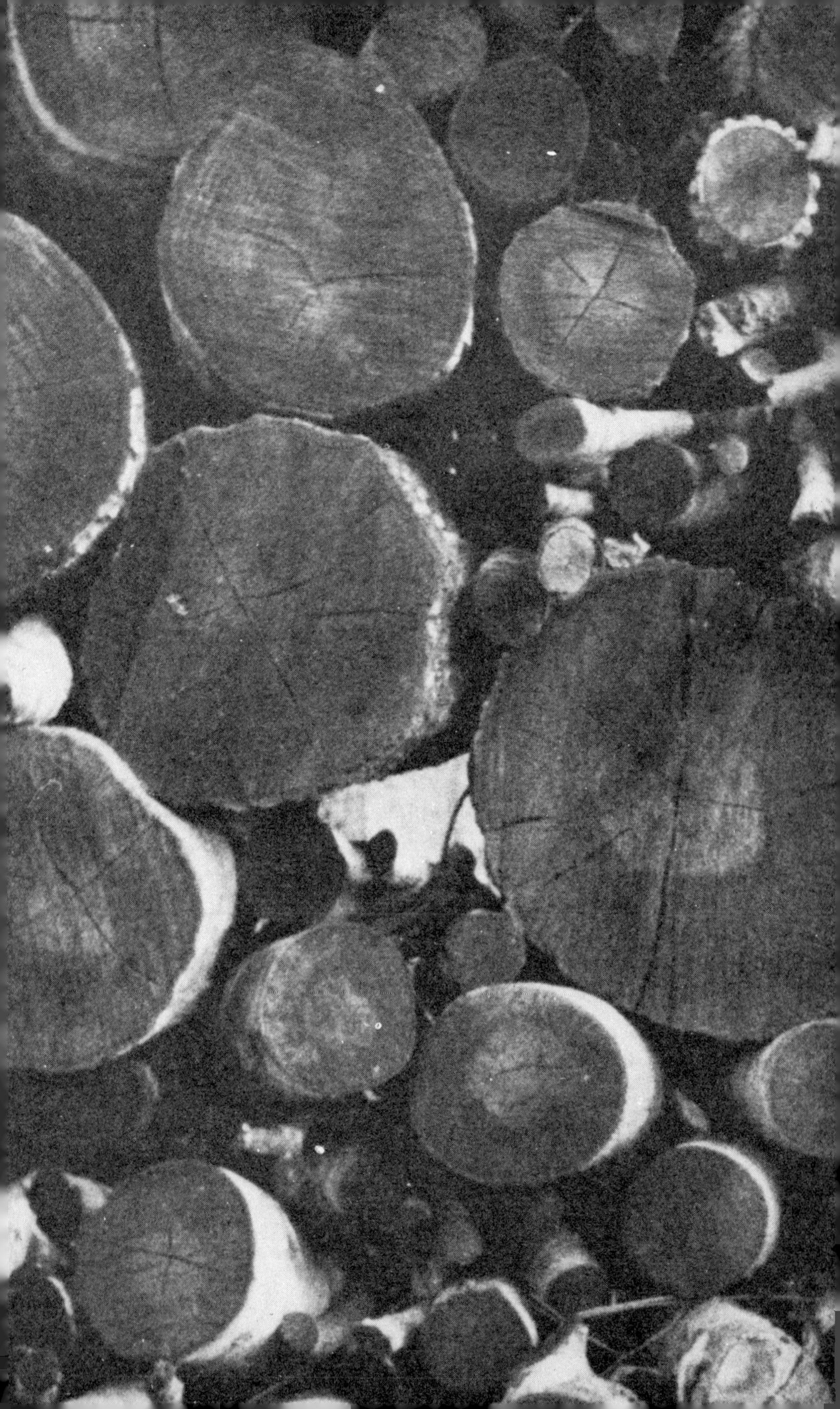

clocks, knows objectively that winter will end some distant day in March—or April or May. But the part of us that feeds on light, our inarticulate and illiterate cells, had nearly despaired of spring. It seemed to the cells that they would drag on through these stench-filled corridors forever, the burden of moribund tissue finally overwhelming the hope of health.

Then at last one day the angle at which the sun's rays strike the earth reaches a particular pitch, imparting to that creaturely light sensor in us, ancient and almost as obsolete as the appendix, that yes! the light does return. Though it be a long way off from dawning, yet inside the dark, close cave we can hear the call: "Lazarus, come out!"

And this second day confirms the first. The wind is whipping the snow over the crests of the Wyoming foothills in a fine white plume set off against a sky as blue as Mary's mantle. This is no gentle spring breeze. It's gale force, and we can scarcely make it to the top of the hill. Our footprints are sifted over again in only a few minutes, obliterating the trace of our witness to any softening of the season. The ice crystals cut into our faces. It is, after all, only the middle of February. But the air, discounting the windchill factor, is slightly above freezing. One can inhale without impairing one's lungs. A first friendly gesture from the atmosphere that had seemed an implacable enemy, and one begins to stir within the swathing of the graveclothes. The wind that seemed before the very breath of bitterness in deadly seriousness is today a joke.

And the light! When has there ever been such a riot of reflection and refraction? The sky rebounds blue upon blue with it. The glaze formed on the snow's melting surface makes a mirror for it. The crystals, whipped like razors through the air, glint, making the wind visible. The blue shadows of the bare aspen on the snow are angled to interlace with the sun's striking, and by this sign the inner sensor *knows* and shuffles once more inside the shroud. "There's light at the end of the tunnel," my husband shouts above the wind, "and it's filled with fish."

I have brought my camera with me into the hills, and, intoxicated by the light, like a trapper I set out to catch it. "Hurry, before the light changes," I tell my friend who is taking the measure of the ponds, still frozen in strangely heaved shapes, for summer possibilities.

A camera is a funny thing. It is, in fact, a tunnel with light at the end of it, that one fills with reflective images. All my inner light sensors grope toward the aperture fastened to my right eye. I ignore the wind, the cold, the snow; only this square of vision exists. I fall on my stomach to shoot up the hillside, filling my boots with snow, staggering through a drifted-over ravine to find a shadow.

But seeing for a camera is different from seeing for yourself. The camera gobbles the light and feeds it into its celluloid entrails. McLuhan was wrong about its being an extension of the eye. In fact, not only the eye but also the whole body becomes an extention of the camera. Like the mouth of an anemone it consumes, consumes, consumes, eating light endlessly. And your arms and legs and brain stalk are merely the antennae waving about, searching out and ensnaring delectables for its voracious appetite. There is no time for reflection with a camera, only absorption. One hustles the light rays of the universe like an unscrupulous, shifty-eyed panhandler, dashing here and there before some scene escapes, oblivious of the self. Sensory impressions are neither savored nor digested but swallowed whole as a boa constrictor consumes its prey.

Still I rush on, so starved have I been for this delectation of light. It is as though my eyeballs have scurvied over from a deficiency of light, and the camera is like a liver where I will hoard the light away against another night.

Finally some friendly gremlin intervenes, however, and jams the film spindle when I try to load another roll. The camera refuses to give up its film, though I jiggle and shake and unscrew. I take a deep breath and give up. All right.

I can never keep this up for long, anyway. For one thing, the very narrowing of the field of vision by the camera's mouth makes me finally unsteady and sick at my stomach. I need my peripheral vision as well as my inner ear for balance.

Memory asserts itself now, insisting on superimposing pictures from the past on those of today. Words float up and attach themselves like barnacles to the underside of sense impressions. It takes time, I find, to transform sheer visual stimuli into experience. I must pace myself in the midst of this rich February day, or I'll have sensory indigestion by its end.

Finding that I can garner no more light, we decide to gather wood instead. Though the snows cover whatever has fallen or blown down, we find some dead standing saplings, cut off from the light by their overshadowing siblings. One good pull, and they snap off from the root. We trail them through the snow back to our car and saw them into fireplace lengths. Not much, but enough for a couple of evenings' memories.

The sun is just below the green black tops of the ponderosa and fir now. Their spear-shaped upper parts shatter the light to either side, making shafts through which the wind-whipped snow swirls in smoky spirals. The closer it gets to sunset, the more winter reasserts itself in the scene. We begin to notice our wet socks and chapped faces. We tumble our gear into the car, hurrying now before the darkness overtakes us.

Still, we have seen the light today. We feel, like Noah's dove, that we are bearing an olive branch back to our ark. We have marked the place when the light struck the earth. From now on the darkness can only recede. The sun, steadied on its beams, will rise higher and higher. It will not slip back, not even for one day, but will move inexorably forward.

Home again before the fireplace we watch the wood we sawed up burning. It is aspen and burns hotter than pine. Even without being split, it catches fire, sending out waves of fine, dry, penetrating heat. It breaks apart, and the light races back and forth across the face of its heart.

What is this fire but emanations of its aspen self, the sunlight stored for seasons in its concentric circles of cells? Now it gives back those years in a swift blast. Here is the light I sought today, a concentrate of sun, transferred through 93,000,000 miles of space to the tentacles of trees and finally to my fireplace. Here an aspen skeleton lies in my grate, evanescing into energy. A chunk of the sun, glowing into gas again. Like Lazarus returning to the light of the world, free of its graveclothes, it rises now.

Through a glass darkly. If we see at all in winter, it is in that diminished mode. The seed that harbors the germ of faith is hidden in dark ground. To bring it forth into fruitfulness requires not just time, the enduring of a few days or months of darkness, but light. We think, mistakenly, that it is the warmth of spring days that brings up the buds. Seeds are not responding to the balmy weather above, however, when they poke their sprouts through the snow. The longer days are what trip the switch on their genetic clocks. It is light that calls them forth, that sets in motion the sluggish starches. Seed or Lazarus, they burst their bonds and rise only at the invitation of the light.

"In thy light do we see light," proclaimed the psalmist. "For with thee is the fountain of life." A fountain of photons showers the spring. They penetrate the earth to a depth of one thousand feet and pierce the human bodies twenty times a second. And old Lazarus stirs expectantly beneath the soil.

Tasting
the World

        For the human species, making sense means making sensible. Every concept, every idea, however ethereal, must be brought, even if only through imagination, into the range of the senses in order for us to understand it. We sometimes speak with reverence about abstract ideas. We harbor feelings of awe and perhaps fear toward those who manipulate such ideas as nimbly as knitting needles, forgetting that such high-flown cognition must first of all be "abstracted" from the concrete, from the tangible, visual, audible, odiferous, delectable world we are all submerged in. There are no notions, no thoughts that do not take their rise here. However high the mental kite flies, it can always be traced back by its string to earth and the realm of our senses.
        Which is not to say that some very real things are not beyond the reach of our senses. And even these invisible, intangible realities we can talk about. But when we do, we must necessarily do so in terms of something we can, in fact, grasp in the tendrils of our nerve endings.
        We don't always like being put in this, our proper place. We'd like to twitch off this mortal mantle at times. We see it, and rightly so, as a limitation. We dream of some mode of apprehending reality directly, without the need for such clumsy, even grotesque instruments as tongues and tympanic membranes.
        The Nobel-laureate physicist, Werner Heisenberg, at one point attempted to dump language altogether in his search for an unassailable description of atomic structure. Especially did he find objectionable the planetary model of the atom proposed by Niels

Bohr in which the nucleus of an atom acts as its sun, about which revolve the planetlike electrons, each in its constantly shifting orbit. However, since the electrons make several million billion such circuits a second, they can just as well be said to form a spherical oscillating shell about the nucleus. Indeed, it proved useful to talk about the electrons first in one way and then in the other. Such ambiguity in language may be intoxicating to poets and their fuzzy-headed admirers, but it was an affront to Heisenberg for whom accuracy was a point of honor. Therefore he proposed, along with his colleague Wolfgang Pauli, to formulate a "unified field theory" of elementary particles or what was soon named a "world formula." Since any word whatever betrays at some point in its ancestry that fatal link to our sensory perception of the physical world, they attempted to describe the orbit of electrons purely in terms of numbers.

He failed to convince his fellow physicists, however, despite the accuracy of his math. Although he had the ancient Greek, Pythagoras, on his side ("All things are numbers."), even his fellow pioneer in quantum mechanics, Pascual Jordan, insisted that ". . . seeing and understanding are inseparably linked. The intellectual conquest of nature is largely accomplished by making visible things that previously were invisible. . . ." Indeed, language, as though determined to have its revenge, has since exploded with the amazing fecundity of a ripe dandelion head in the sciences, particularly in physics where words such as "spin" and "strange" have been revitalized with exotic meanings and new words like "quark" invented. All this while "unified field theory" has been engorged by those embarrassing siblings of physics, the social sciences, whose legitimacy is still very much in question.

Scientists, however hard they hew to the severely classic line, cannot force themselves to renounce the process of picturing what they are talking about. Indeed, the overwhelming desire of even a physicist to *see* what his numbers have predicted brought about the invention of the electron microscope, a device that makes the truly invisible visible or at least photographable.

We can know *about* numbers, even manipulate them with considerable skill. But we do not know *in* numbers. We perceive in pictures. And in squeezes and pungency and bites and bitterness.

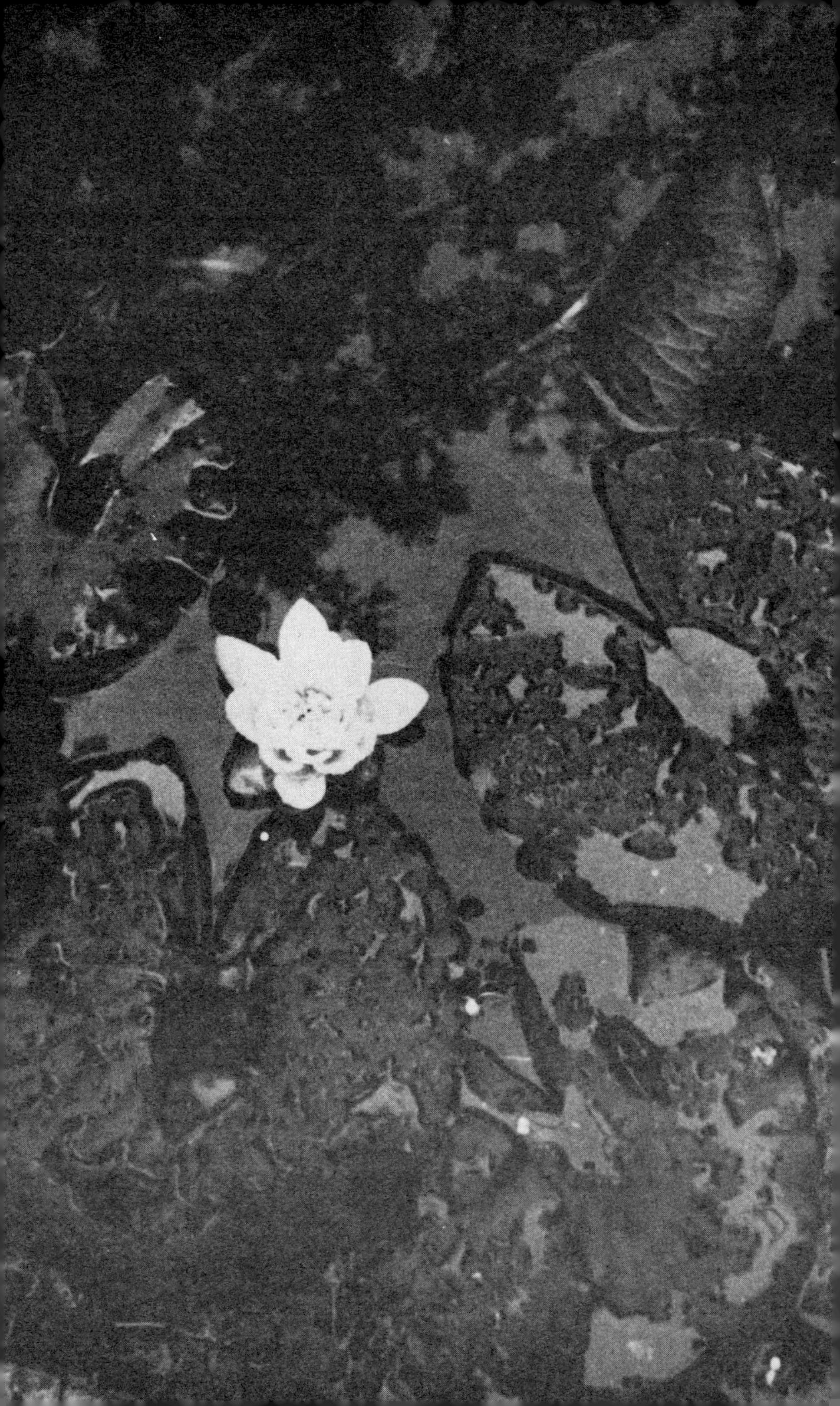

That is our fate as humans. Even what we call "intuitive" knowledge is the direct appropriation of sensory data without its being processed into words and symbols. This wordless witnessing of the world, the way a preliterate child does, is something we are never quite rid of, however high the wall of words we build between ourselves and primary reality.

When we grow ashamed of our senses, we grow guilty of that aspiration that some have called "angelism." However, C. S. Lewis says:

> But for our body, one whole realm of God's glory—all that we receive through the senses—would go unpraised. For the beasts can't appreciate it and the angels are, I suppose, pure intelligences. They *understand* colours and tastes better than our greatest scientists; but have they retinas or palates? I fancy the "beauties of nature" are a secret God has shared with us alone. That may be one of the reasons why we were made—and why the resurrection of the body is an important doctrine.

We used to write plays warning ourselves of the fate of Faust who wanted to saturate his senses and who sold his soul to do it. Now the danger lies in the opposite direction; it comes from those who would annihilate the senses in order to achieve some sort of either scientific or soulful spiritualism. They are as fully prepared to trade off their nerve endings as Faust was his soul if in turn they are granted some purer plane of apprehension.

To be a human being is to occupy that peculiar niche in creation that can see from just above the infrared range on the light spectrum to just below the ultraviolet. But certain ones of us, seeking to perceive through angels' eyes, will ingest certain chemicals that break down the molecular arrangement of our own brain cells in the hopes of watching the atoms dance, of turning our own rather limited retinas into electron microscopes.

It is the soul that modern heretics would immortalize, though they would perhaps call it something else; the body, they think, should stay decently buried. With its ridiculous, sensing protuberances it has become a theological embarrassment.

Science has been astoundingly clever in inventing devices that extend the sense organs past their limitations in the raw state. But in theology the recent thrust has too often been to spiritualize the physical out of perceptible existence. Blood and body, light and darkness. All these are seen as mere rough metaphors for delicate concepts of pure meaning. After all, is not the metaphysical composed of a more diaphanous tissue than the merely physical? Our knowledge of God, goes the Heisenbergian argument, can no more be chained to such rough approximations as an avenging warrior or a wooing lover than knowledge of matter can be sought in waves and corpuscles.

". . . [We] know in part," declares Paul. This is precisely what drives us crazy in the twentieth century. The limitation of our power of knowledge is the primary concern of philosophers, politicians, physicists, and journalists. Who can know how much of what and by what means; this is our obsession. Almost everyone seems to have lost sight of *why* we should know anything at all—whether little or much. Why should we have even the three color receptors on our retinas? Would an ability to see cosmic rays make clear the purpose of green, or would the multiplication of perception only make it more mystifying? The question is not how much of the world we are able to apprehend, but what is the point of perception itself?

Helen Keller's humanness was not diminished because of her sensory impairment. In fact, her very deficiencies heightened her perception of tactile vibrations to the point where her body was a veritable barometer, sensing changes in atmospheric pressure. Her body became an exceedingly finely adjusted tuning fork, quivering with delight as it registered wave upon wave in a surging ocean of creation. Honing made her more human, not less. She embraced her limitation, which is to say her definition, with joy in the specialized knowledge it gave her.

For knowledge is necessary to praise. That is the why of our senses. Not the mere accumulation of endless information. Libraries, telescopes, cyclotrons, satellites, encyclopedias—all the gear of human knowing is for this end. If not, Helen Keller's story is nonsensical.

Why should the discovery of the birthday bang of the universe fill scientific—which only means knowing—creatures with excitement? Why is it not merely one more bit of data compiled and stored? Information alone holds no thrills. Could this excitement not be some far distant shock wave still reverberating around the universe, an echo of the pleasure that praise gives creatures prepared for precisely that function? Perception and praise. Two sides of the coin of the realm of heaven. "O taste and see that the LORD is good!" More information has not altered our basic humanity from that of the psalmist. We are still essentially the same as a race, and it is the capacity for perceiving and for praising that maintains this kinship over the centuries. No amount of information can alter what it means to be human, although it may extend the scope of our essential activity.

The Bible speaks constantly of the "knowledge of God," and what is meant is quite obviously not an analytical dissection of deity. It is neither the sort of knowledge Eve sought and gained in the garden, to our everlasting sorrow, nor is it the knowledge the tower builders of Babel unsuccessfully sought in piercing heaven. It is not, in other words, power over God.

Because we have discovered certain facts about the nature of light, we can bend it with magnets, sift it with crystals, even blot it out with interfering waves of the same frequency. But manipulation is not the main point unless one's ultimate commitment is to technology. Even among scientists there remains this rudimentary dichotomy between "pure" and "applied" science. The purist defends his probing of the cosmos, one could almost say, religiously. He senses that fingering the material of the universe for any merely utilitarian purpose is somehow shabby. To make shop goods of the cosmos cramps the elegance of his style.

Thus are the arts and sciences fitly yoked. The purpose of both is pleasure. Although the delight arises from the exercise of different aspects of our human capacities, its object is always praise. The laboratory as well as the stage is a place of toil that ends in exuberance. Whee! Eureka! At last! Hallelujah! Bravo! The ejaculations of the overflowing human spirit, whether powered by music or microscopes, are releases of undeniable gladness. Some, knowing their true source, are like homing pigeons making straight for the center. Others, unsure of their destination, may wander about like Noah's raven. But the very fact of such a sudden, spontaneous utterance—even made thoughtlessly, a burst of pure pleasure seeking its source—is a sign of hope. And a sign of humanity.

The Primal Metaphor

It is not information we seek as humans, but illumination, that sudden irradiation of our understanding that has no real relationship to the accretion of data. We have known since 1897 about the photoelectric effect of light on matter, a shower of electric charges liberated from a material bombarded with radiant energy. But illumination, sudden and sometimes shattering insight, has been a part of our experience ever since we began recording it.

Light, even in a society that prides itself on its ignorant relativism, remains our Absolute. At its speed, matter not only disappears but also stops, its absolute mass suspended in time. Sleeping Beauty, before the prince's time-warping kiss, was traveling at the speed of 186,242 miles per second. Eternity is not then an empty concept, the foolish invention of stasis-seekers. Eternity races toward us from the sun by day and the stars by night. It is the first thing God created when he spoke light into being. We bathe in it, work by it, even feed on it. Deprived of it, our very bones grow rickety; our liver and kidneys fail. Without this constant supply of eternity bombarding our planet and being stored away by chloroplasts, temporal life would be impossible. Light is not simply a metaphor for all sorts of nebulous and esoteric experiences. It is not just the light bulb flashing on over the head of the cartoon character or the halo behind the saint or the Quaker's inner spark.

Photons are themselves phenomena. This is where the metaphor comes true, where it is at once symbol and substance. Here the finger touches the object it points to.

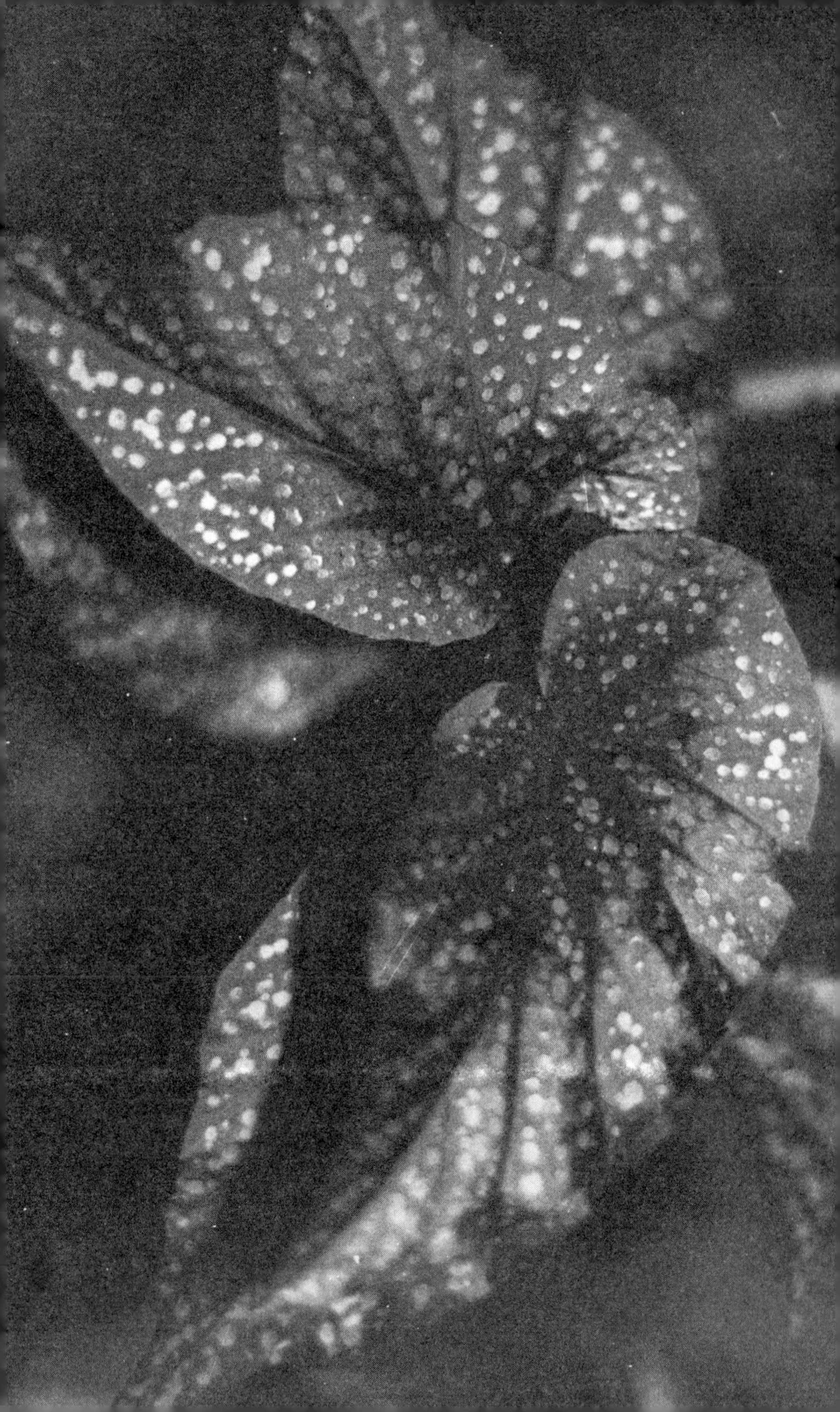

Our intellectual sensitivities may be annoyed by the indiscriminate use of metaphors from nature to describe our experiences. "Life is like a stream." With Heraclitus it might have been fresh, but centuries later it is only hackneyed and ho-hum. The village blacksmith may in certain ways be like a mighty oak, but spare us the similes today. Ever since the Enlightenment and the rise of science as a religion, we have grown increasingly unable to bear hearing human life spoken about in terms of natural objects. Now we are growing positively allergic to the ineradicable tendency of language to compare offhandedly one natural object to another. Hence, Heisenberg's aversion to light "waves" or the electron's "orbit."

But light itself, elusive in its actual nature, is what has put a stop to this puritanical drive to purge at least scientific language from its deplorable tendency toward messy metaphorism. Light, capricious and changeable, is now motion, now matter. If it is to be talked about at all, it simply must be described in terms of something it never dogmatically is. That is its very nature.

Isaac Asimov, that prodigious author of over two hundred books which have made available to the laity all the discovered delights of the universe usually reserved to specialists, grows a little touchy about light's elusive nature. "This has been made to seem a paradox, or even a kind of mysticism, as if the true nature of light passes all possible understanding," he complains in *The New Intelligent Man's Guide to Science*. Yet in order to explain the operation of demythologized light, he has to fall back on making a rather murky analogy of light with a man who "may have many aspects: husband, father, friend, businessman. Depending on circumstances and on his surroundings, he behaves like a husband, father, friend, or businessman, . . . and yet that makes him neither a paradox nor more than one man." Asimov could perhaps learn something about the more elegant application of analogies from the fourth-century church fathers' working out of the doctrine of the Trinity. The fact that he would draw such parallels at all between the behavior of light and that of a man, far from clearing up any little misunderstandings we might have had on the subject, only makes the whole matter ultimately more mystic than ever. Why should light "behave" at all? Why should it present to us now one profile, now another?

The true nature of light. No, it is not past all possible understanding. Even Lucretius, two thousand years ago, did not prove to be totally wrong. "Know then that bodies have, as we call them, their semblances which are slender membranes detaching themselves from their surface and flying in every direction in the air. . . . These semblances must traverse incalculable distances in a flash; first because they are exceedingly small elements, and there is behind them a cause which thrusts them forward; and secondly they fly in swarms so subtle that they can easily penetrate and as it were pour through the air." During the time when light was thought to be only waves—pure motion—Lucretius was discredited as another ignorant ancient. But Prince Louis de Broglie, another Nobel Prize winner, found Lucretius's speculation about these rarified corpuscles of light consistent with the quantum theory and was amazed at "the profundity of this intuition."

It is, indeed, the "true nature of light" that has been the secret sought by scientists for scores of centuries. For the nature of everything else created seems to be revealed only by passing through this most primeval form of creation. Even the current theory of the origin of life upon this planet relies on light, perhaps lightning, to have assembled and organized the necessary components out of a miasma of vapors. And the most accurate means of identifying any of the chemical elements of which the universe is composed is through spectroscopy. Substances are heated to the point of incandescence; their glow is spread out by prisms into spectra, and the characteristic colors of the elements are identified. In other words, the kind of light an element gives out is what identifies it. *Spectrum* means, in Latin, "ghost," and it is the pure spirit of matter itself that is thus revealed. Glowing sodium, for example, produces a yellow light, while lithium salt is, by spectral analysis, a brilliant red.

The world is, in fact, made of light, as Einstein's famous equation shows. Energy is convertible into mass and vice versa. And what is more amazing, none is ever lost, however long the seesaw process goes on. Matter may evanesce into motion, or energy may be compacted into "the jittery to-and-fro trembling of molecules in solids" (Asimov's own admirable description), but none of it gets blown away, dropped, spilled, or wasted. Such conservation of energy, which is only another word for light both visible and invisible, must satisfy the souls of radical environmentalists and Republicans alike.

Only light can have a true nature. Perhaps that is, after all, the important point. Although generations of schoolchildren have no doubt been frustrated by the definition of dark as the absence of light (and that of cold as the absence of heat), that is the nearest one can come to the truth about the dark and cold. Light is a "thing" in a way dark is not. There are neither waves nor corpuscles of darkness. Saint Augustine's explanation of evil provokes a parallel here. Just as darkness is not a thing in itself but an absence, a void, so evil is not the created counterpart to good. Only goodness, like light, has being. The diminishing of that being is what we call in one case evil and in the other case darkness. As long as some form of being continues, both goodness and light continue. Small wonder that humanity has always connected light with goodness, truth, understanding. The bottom of Dante's hell is not fire, which gives both heat and light, but ice, a frozen lake. And his heaven is merely a movement from lesser light to greater until one reaches the source:

> That light doth so transform a man's whole bent
> That never to another sight or thought
> Would he surrender, with his own consent;
> For everything the will has ever sought
> Is gathered there, and there is every quest
> Made perfect. . . .

It would seem that one must be of a most willfully obstinate nature to resist this witness of ubiquitous light, ever present, from the conflagration of the nebulae to the sheerest scoring of a photographic plate by a positron. How can we hold it in the mind and not be undone by the wonder of it, losing our minds somewhere in the intricate maze of this mandala? To be a body, penetrated by light, whose photoreceptors drink it in, whose face shines by means of ricocheting photons—such participation in the phenomenon of radiant energy should only happen to creatures capable of joy in this marvel.

Yet it seems to raise only the most primitive spirits in us. And most of the time we are merely concerned with snipping little bits out of this fabric of creation in order to make ourselves little gewgaws we call technology. We can't even approach the point of seeing the universe as art because we are so obsessed with turning it into tools. If we could learn to believe ourselves primarily praise singers instead of problem solvers, perhaps the perceptions of our spirits could be heightened to the point where they could at least equal our retinas. Clumsy cyclotrons could be augmented by apprehending, as John did, "the true light that enlightens every man. . . ."

But mankind as a species is still bent on solving problems rather than singing praises. The vital connection between matter and what we were made for has been broken. And that is why, as C. S. Lewis observed, "A true philosophy may sometimes validate an experience of nature; an experience of nature cannot validate a philosophy. . . . Nature never taught me that there exists a God of glory and of infinite majesty. I had to learn that in other ways. But nature gave the word *glory* a meaning for me. I still do not know where else I could have found one."

Making the connection between glory and God. That is what light does. There first has to be that second creation, that other flash of lightning that reveals to our marred vision what should be as natural as rain, as obvious as the air we breathe. "To this end was I born, and for this cause came I into the world, that I should bear witness unto the truth." This is the illumination we long for—the Light of the world himself. And the truth that he illumines is our own true destiny: that we ourselves are children of light, intended for glory.

The Importance of Purple

I try to get home to East Texas at least once a year, usually in the spring. It runs there, like a well-applauded play, from early March to the first of June when Wyoming is still buried under winter. All things partake of a certain tenderness then. Even the light, though it may toughen and scorch the earth by August, in March and April trembles in the air like a distillation of the purest photons. I can almost remember, in such light, what it was that made me, as a child, open *my* eyes in the morning, eager for rising. Everything rises easily in that amiable atmosphere—seeds, tree tips, birds, clouds, scents, and spirits. Snakes and night crawlers thaw out and wriggle up from their holes. Insect pupae grow wings and dry them delicately in the light. The earth exhales and expands. The very origin of the season's name in Old English means "a place of rising." Like Lazarus, freed from the graveclothes of darkness and death, creation leaps toward the light.

It is easy in such seasons to see the world as a sign. Each green leaf becomes an allegory of grace. If in harsher, hostile atmospheres we are inclined to cynicism over an easy every-little-blade-of-grass theology, nevertheless one hyacinth poking through the black earth makes our knees weak enough to kneel.

"Why?" we shout upward at the light quivering just above the treetops. Why should a hyacinth be such a shattering shade of purple? Why should the lilies of the field be arrayed so gloriously if not to woo us? Why, indeed? Only a Prufrock, wandering in the wasteland of winter, careful of breaking his heart, finds April the cruelest month.

Those of us who are foolish enough to be willing to have our hearts pounded to a pulp year after year insist that the fact that leaves are green and blossoms purple *means* something. And not just to the bees gathering pollen whose perception of color is much more limited even than ours. Where even a dullard can distinguish sixty shades of color, a bee responds to only four. Thus the infinite varieties of merely purple are not necessary for maximum insect efficiency.

That the skin on an East Texas redbud tree should be silver is a hieroglyphic of an incalculable language, obviously connected by some spiritual syntax to the buds, somewhere between fuschia and flesh, that open even before the later heart-shaped leaves. The redbud tree is a whole letter in itself, a Rosetta stone that I, for one, would be willing to devote a lifetime to deciphering.

The Protestant side of my soul draws up the pagan at this point, however. Forever sniffing for sacrilege, it demands an explanation of its Siamese twin. It smells the breath for signs of drinking dewdrops in a pantheistic toast to creation. For this seeking of signs among the spring things is very near, if not to deifying a few sprouts, at least to sacramentalizing them. Meaning that if they are not God himself, they are in some way his word to us.

"Well," the pagan side answers back defiantly, "why not?" (He is a little grubby with dirt under his fingernails and only bathes under duress. "Still," his Protestant twin sighs, "he has vigor and one wonders what this child of Adam might have been had not. . . .") So they sit down together, the two sides of my soul—the unkempt, odiferous, gleaming-eyed pagan on the ground and the starched, strong, wistful Protestant on a stump—and attempt to reason this matter out.

"And matter," declares the Protestant, "is precisely the problem. You, Pagan, take it too seriously, and it misleads you. What you need is to learn how to read—and not redbud trees either, but words. Real words. You see, with language I can draw off the essential liquor of whatever it is you love in nature: life, growth, constancy, beauty, power. What is left is only Esau's potage, sensuality that enslaves the spirit."

The Protestant twin smiles benignly on his illiterate sibling who is frowning darkly, obviously groping for words to answer this. He closes his eyes to concentrate, but all he can envision is a terrapin he

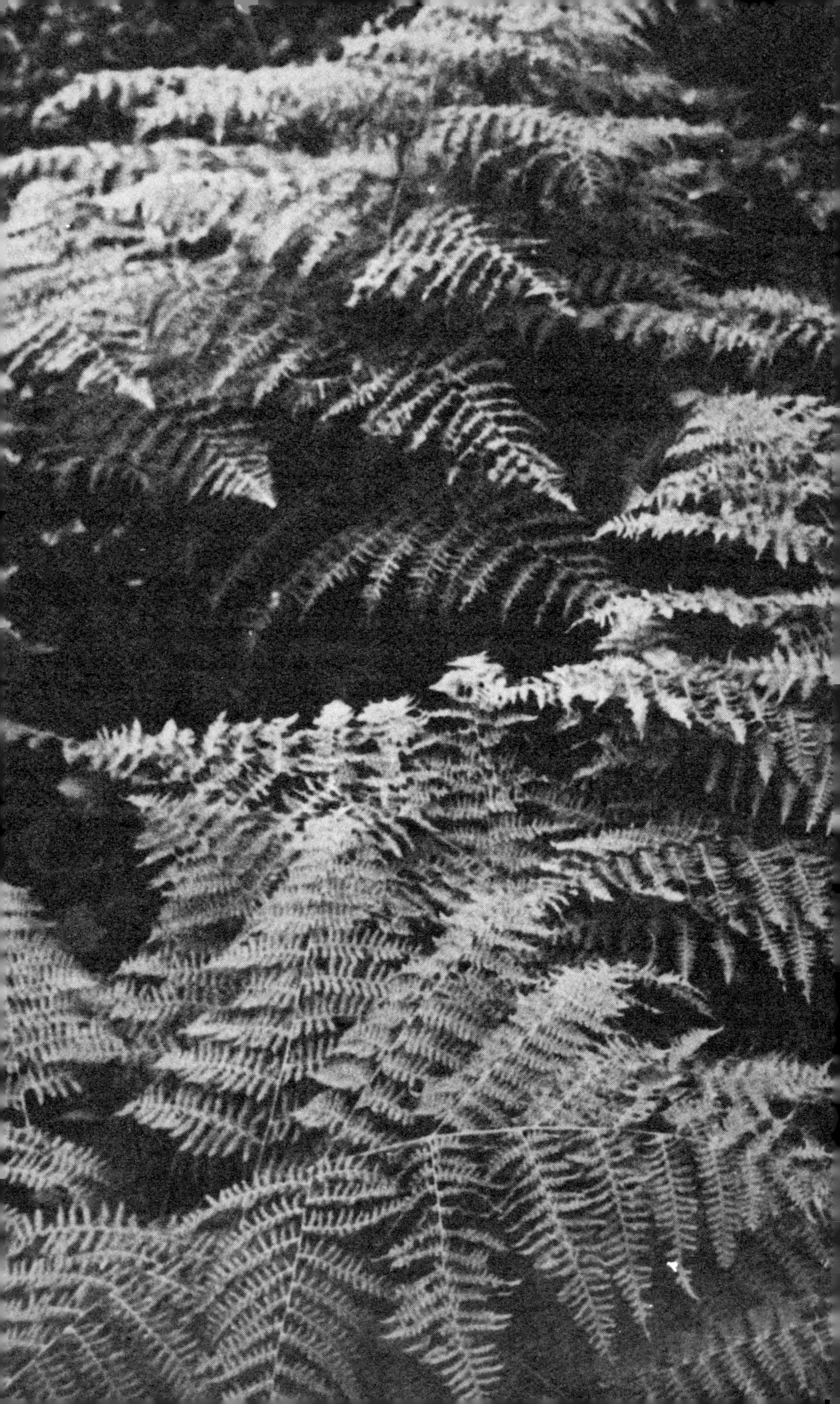

saw in the woods that morning, its head a deep and glossy coral with a black eye that blinked once before it drew itself into its shell. That color of coral was like life itself, shockingly protruding from the gray green inert shell. And then there was the tallow tree, its yellow drooping catkins fragrant and bee swarmed. The dew, trickling from leaf to leaf, collecting in pools in the hollow next the stem till its weight reached the critical point where it spilled in a splattering, split-second shower. He remembers a spider web anchored on one side to a rotting stump and stretched out across aromatically decaying leaves with a tunnel pulled tight in the middle like a nylon stocking. The pagan's mind is like a riverbed over which pour these memories, glinting as they run. How can he tell his twin that he was arrested at the sight of the terrapin, how his foot hung in the air while he stared and stared and the creature blinked? How can he explain the sudden release inside himself as the weight of the water ricocheted downward from leaf to leaf or why he sat hunkered over the spider tunnel, waiting for its weaver to appear?

How indeed, since he himself doesn't know? All he knows is that his heart was like a great molten marble of desire in his tightening thorax, like the rose exploding in the green gecko's throat outside his window. He was filled with desire and exaltation and the peace of being among things bent on being themselves. But all he can say to his twin is, "Terrapin!" and "Tree!" and "Spider!"

"Aha!" Protestant replies, raising a vertical forefinger. "You see? That's how it always ends: exchanging 'the glory of the immortal God for images resembling mortals or birds or animals or reptiles.' Worshiping the creature rather than the Creator."

Pagan scowls yet more darkly. *That's not what I meant at all,* he thinks.

And on Protestant's face also there is something of a small frown. He is nothing if not scrupulous, and he, too, is remembering. But he remembers in words, the words that preceded his admonishing quotation to his erring twin. "Ever since the creation of the world his invisible nature, namely, his eternal power and deity, has been clearly perceived in the things that have been made." Now stretching power and deity to terrapins and spiders seems a bit farfetched, although he does suppose one could get a notion of grandeur from the Grand Canyon. One would have to assume that the Creator of the universe would necessarily be bigger than his own creation. But, unfortunately, it didn't seem to work in such a reasonable way. One ended up with a sacred ibis or a sacred cow. Dark frenzies mirroring the mating of heaven and earth. Ecstasies of death dripping human blood. It is this he wishes he could make clear to his twin, for he loves him, albeit condescendingly. However, there is no use clouding the issue at this point. What he needs, nay, is obliged to do, is to alert Pagan to the dangers of giving too much attention to creation. For attention soon leads to allegiance, he has found.

"Consider," he begins again, in a conciliatory tone.

"The lilies of the field," Pagan interjects, his dark eyes lighting up.

"No, no, no." Protestant is taken aback at being thus caught up with words. "That's another thing altogether. What I was going to say is, observe, for example, the effect scientism has had on our century. The very ones who took it upon themselves to investigate creation are also the ones who have given us the means of despising and destroying it. Do you think creation is to them a sacrament?"

Pagan, however, is still scratching his frowsy head over the word "investigate." That makes it sound as though creation were a crime perpetrated on our consciousness. No. "Consider" is still the word for him. It was considering he had been doing, face-to-face with the terrapin.

"And ecologists and environmentalists," Protestant goes on, warming to his subject, "although they may think they are counteracting the deleterious effects of their fellow scientists, are only abdicating the most difficult task of all by instead adjudicating the conflicting claims of snail darters and whooping cranes. They have not yet faced the central anthropological issue: that man alone in all of nature is insane, and that the only way to save the planet from his ferocity is either by extinction or redemption."

Pagan is in utter confusion by now. All he can remember is something about a certain shade of purple. He knows that it is this he must cling to, this damson film, his only shred of protection against his twin's frosty words. The purple is important.

Of course, the purple he sees is not a disembodied splotch of color, floating in outer darkness before his inner eye. That is the way Protestant perceives purple, but not Pagan. It is part of a particular tissue, turgid with sap. And in the sap, some antisacramental scientist could tell him, is dissolved both alkali and anthocyanin, chemicals whose cominglings produce the purple before which Pagan is prepared to prostate himself. It would please him to know that the purple is liquid, running just below the translucent skin of the cell. There is something in the paradox of hydraulic pressure, the fact that water, a shapeless volume, should be the means to make the stalk stand upright and the petals curl, that amuses him. *Someone has been very clever here,* he snickers to himself. But he is not prepared to rip open the skin to show the sap beneath or to watch it go limp in his hand to prove a point. Although he could quite possibly eat it, stuffing the stem, leaves, petals, and pollen all at once into his mouth, licking the juice from his lips.

It is a wild creature, this pagan side of my soul. It is capable of extravagant mistakes in its exuberance for experiencing the world. Its awe and wonder over pigmented petals is easily perverted. It has been painful to Pagan to learn that the mystery which moves in them is elusive to him. The terrapin pulls in his coral head; the spider will not come out of his tunnel; the purple recedes from the petals which fall and disintegrate. Yet they have not told him a thing. Except that someone has been very clever here. They have their faces turned away from him, looking somewhere else. Of all the tropisms in creation, there seems to be no anthropotropism.

Yet the mystery continues to absorb Pagan, and he keeps alive the essential questions: Why don't birds worry? What kind of beings are animals? Why so many shades of purple? Where do fires go when they go out? Questions the investigators turned their backs on long ago when creation ceased to be a sign. Questions Protestant suspects are silly and stupid and cannot quite take seriously.

He and the investigators at least speak the same language, although they hallow different words. They both build mental structures amazing in their virtuosity. I often wonder why it was that *they* were not linked together in a Siamese state. For Pagan builds nothing at all. He only wonders and considers. It seems my soul is unequally yoked together. And it makes for some hard and staggered pulling at times.

Yet I suspect that neither of them is ever going to get very far without the other, although a great deal of their time is spent sitting there fruitlessly, Pagan scowling resentfully at Protestant's harangues. Pagan by himself would be left with a sad futility. He gropes after the pearly light of an East Texas spring, hoping by his inhalations to understand it. But it is a sacrament without knowledge.

". . . I am only trying to describe the enormous emotions which cannot be described. And the strongest emotion was that life was as precious as it was puzzling," wrote G. K. Chesterton, my soul's matchmaker. "The test of all happiness is gratitude; and I felt grateful, though I hardly knew to whom."

That is what Pagan needs from Protestant—the knowing to whom to be grateful. Perhaps the terrapin could tell him, if terrapins weren't estranged from us. But the terrapin has his face turned toward some other source.

The Pauline Prognosis

For some reason we, like all other living creatures, are crazy for snuffling out every last bit of data about our environment. Even interiorly, leukocytes stream through our circulatory system on a monomaniacal hunt for certain peculiar antigens they are genetically programmed to detect. And as more massive organisms, we display the same sort of behavior but with a larger, more ambiguous prey in mind. It is not a single antigen we are trained to hunt but a whole universe we feel driven to reconnoiter. There is all that *stuff* out there, and if we can succeed in spindling it into our computers, it is bound to tell us . . . something. We have no real sense of what shape the answer will be when we find it, but we feel certain, at least most of the time, that it will be immediately recognizable. It will say, for example, "Here is the pattern, the map of all matter, and here, where you see the X, is where you fit into it."

This kind of human activity has been going on, according to Paul, "ever since the creation of the world." And also according to Paul, it alone hasn't gotten us very far. In spite of the fact that the implications of our investigations should be perfectly obvious to us, we seem to have a burned-out spot somewhere on our retinas and on whatever other receptors we use to engorge this information. The Pauline prognosis is this: that we are futile in our thinking, and our minds are darkened. Paul, of course, has a penchant for stating the case as strongly as possible.

Yet we are not deterred by this assessment of our situation. We go on fumbling after facts, building electron microscopes, cyclotrons,

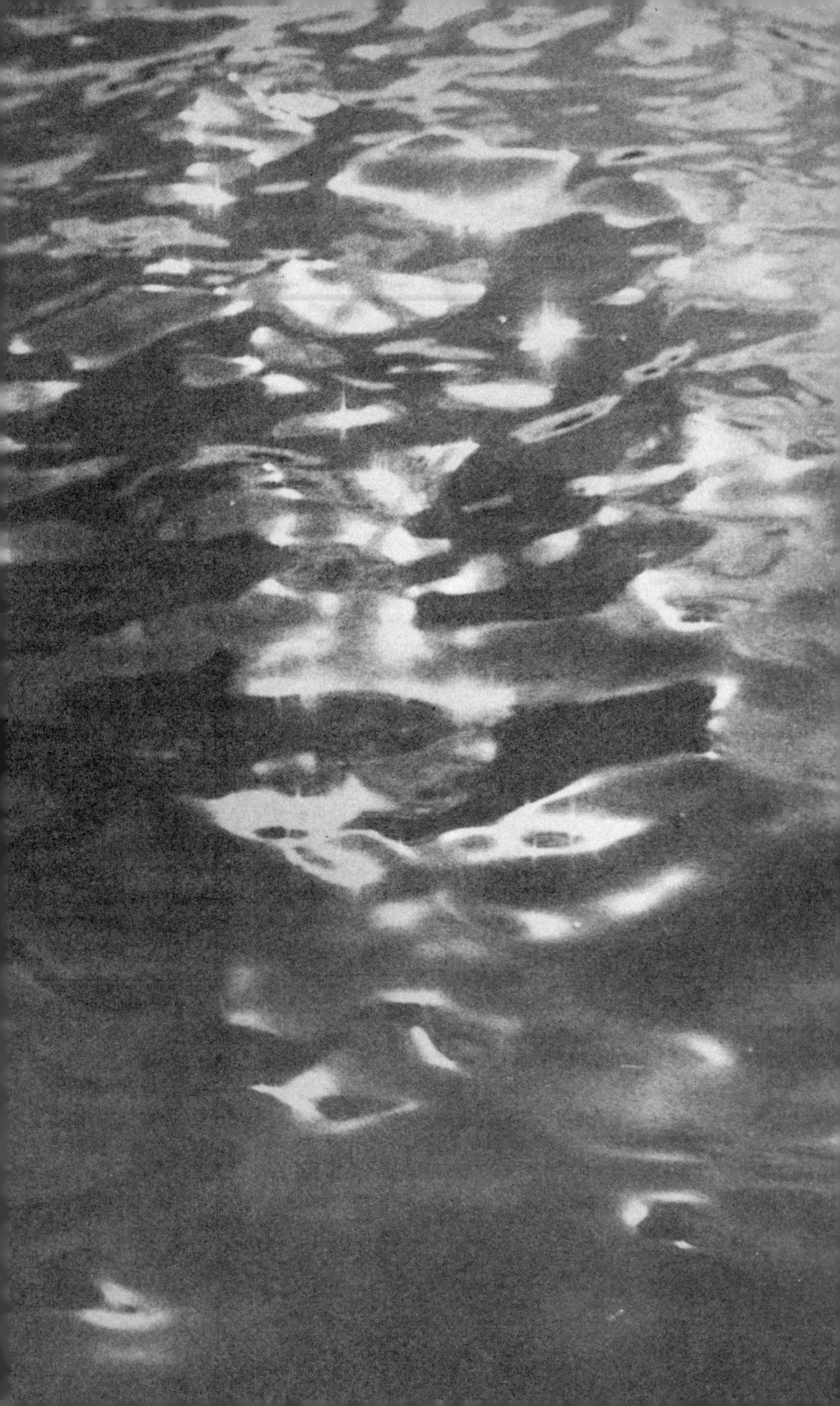

radio telescopes, trying to discover, despite the relatively recent ban on natural theology, what is the nature of Nature. It is a friendly face we search for among the stars. But someone has gotten his genetic wires crossed, for we keep getting hung up on missed connections, exchanging "the glory of the immortal God for images resembling mortal man or birds or animals or reptiles." Unlike the leukocytes, which never miss, whose homing sense is unerring, we are always missing the mark, that friendly face. Or perhaps we are actually afraid of finding it.

At any rate, one clear and lucid piece of evidence has emerged from centuries spent corporately observing our surroundings, and it seems as good a place as any to begin. The evidence is that moral imperatives exist only inside human society which is, after all, a very small segment of creation. Ants and antibodies are not moral creatures, despite the former's frequent appearance in fables. Ants and antibodies, bees and bacteria are *driven*. Their encoded information will not be denied. They *cannot* break the laws of their own natures. Sometimes this seems an abhorrent position to be in, sometimes enviable, depending probably on our current level of energy and capacity for coping. But it is clear, however much we long for it or dread it, that it is not our position.

Moral laws are the only ones that can be broken. Every other part of creation is destined to be stolidly law-abiding. We alone in nature are unnatural—Paul's description of our predicament. We are the bandits, the outlaws, the brigands, simply because we are the only ones who *can* be. Certainly there are patterns that govern human behavior, that, if followed, provide the best climate for the full functioning of our capacities. But we have yet to see in our history these patterns followed with anything like the exactitude of bees locking in on a polarized light beam.

In other words, we, unlike all other creatures with operating instructions written right into their chromosomes, are free. We can contribute to the general good of the organism we call society, or we can disrupt it or even, given wide enough range and a running start, destroy it. And withdrawing behind the lines of society to the individual unit we call our selves, we find that the latest information we have about our heretofore unrecognized authority over our own autonomous nervous systems says it is greater than we'd dreamed.

The ability to control our colon, our heart valves, our sweat glands can, indeed, be expanded. We have only just begun to explore this aspect of our freedom. Mary Baker Eddy has been transformed into biofeedback which everyone takes today with sober seriousness.

Why should we, of all creatures, not participate in the general precision that hums away like an astrolabe? All the universe is dancing, from giant novas to single-celled algae, making graceful gravitational alliances or spinning out in elegant centrifugal curvetes. Where one retreats, the other advances. The intricacy of the pattern is past our imagining. Yet we are the wallflowers, witnessing from the sidelines the skill and grace of this revolving, pulsating choreography we call creation. What makes us wallflowers? What causes our clumsiness when we attempt a few steps on the sidelines? Our very freedom. The ability to decide. Even the frozen-with-fear inability to decide makes us carom around the floor like badly trained elephants.

Feeding one another, reproducing ourselves, processing information—all the ordinary routine of living creatures is done more efficiently and with less blundering about by chimpanzees than by us humans. Any animal society is better organized than ours. No primate in his right mind would ever consider evolving into man, providing he had that worst of all possible curses, a choice. Is it only our anthropoid arrogance that has posited that sort of possibility, has made up the myth of evolution?

To my way of thinking, whatever shreds of automatic behavior we have left should be carefully preserved as that. The fact that my heart can beat without my having to tell it to do so is a great blessing. The liver, the glands, the pancreas, and spleen are the parts of me that can still take part in that carefree choreography of creation. I certainly don't want to go mucking about with them now; they are my last link to the faint echo of that celestial music.

Law, that poor makeshift affair Paul talks about, is what we who have lost our natural rhythm must rely on. It is only a rickety substitute for the natural grace of a loping giraffe or the unerring aim of a photon. Law is a crutch for an amputated limb that makes our attempts at dancing awkward at best. When in whatever primordial situation we insisted on making our own decision about what steps to take, we gave up that easy encoding that makes the rest of creation seem so agile and effortless in comparison. And we took in its place this wooden limb of the law. It enables us to get along in a haphazard fashion. Indeed, life without it would be unthinkable, immobilized. But the fact remains patently obvious: We were intended for better things. The rest of the world doesn't have to hobble along, depending on an artificial limb that is both necessary and despised.

I don't think the human race should get nearly so puffed up about our morality as we do. We have made a virtue out of our amputation and artificial limb. Paul has only the most mediocre things to say in favor of the law. He emphasizes its second-best nature. It is not a product he pushes, as do too many contemporary religious organs. Indeed, he is much more a purveyor of gifts of the Spirit. If he had been a twentieth-century biochemist instead of a first-century social anthropologist and more concerned with microbes than Macedonians, he might have written Romans 2:14-15 like this: "When bacteria who have no morality do by nature what is required of them, they are a law to themselves, even though they are unaware of it. They show that what the law of the universe requires is written in their genes." When we begin to tout our morality as the finest thing about the species, the very paramecia no doubt flutter their cilia in embarrassment for us. For moral law is, in fact, no more than the all-too-evident sign of our askewness with the universe, the lumbering gait with which we stump about the world.

But what of love, this love that Paul calls the greatest of that triumvirate that also includes hope and faith? As we go groping about, engorging information gleaned from our environment, where do we find love? Or hope or faith for that matter? Certainly not in our morality, although we have a loose way of lumping love and law together just because they are both beneficial. But some of the most moral folk the world has known, namely the Stoics, made quite a point of their hopelessness. Nor does morality demand that one believe in what he cannot see. One can demand, and enforce the demand, that we not murder one another or appropriate property indiscriminately. The laws governing the symbiosis of bacteria in the colon may work much more smoothly than our own moral and legal code, but in some inferior fashion we usually manage to avert complete chaos in human societies. However, to make a rule that everyone keep hoping is both ridiculous and unenforceable. Likewise with love.

So where does that leave love? If it is truly the force that makes the world go round, where does one detect traces of it in the environment? If it is not to be found in the artificial limb we call morality, is it a part of our encoded information, our autonomic choiceless systems that operate like our liver? But love, for us, must always be laboriously chosen; there is little about it that, at least at this point in our history, is spontaneous. Though we would be speculating to talk of love among the lower forms of life, at least there is less evidence of outright malice, even in microbes, than in human society. Their chromosomes are not crooked in that particular way.

If it is the nature of Nature we are exploring, it would seem that she is a great deal more good-natured than we are. The British zoologist, Maurice Burton, in his book *Just Like an Animal,* attempts to determine whether any species other than man can be said to act altruistically. He goes so far as to distinguish carefully between "true" altruism (our sort) and so-called genetic altruism. His conclusion is open-ended, since the hypothesis is impossible of experimental proof. Still, even his evidence of behavior brought about by molecular instructions is enough to shame our own feeble efforts. Fidelity among snow geese, for example, far outstrips human marriage statistics. But then they haven't that terrible freedom to overcome.

Still, the fact that snow geese mate for life is a trace of something, I think. The heavens do declare the glory of God, if we can learn the language. If it is only in retrospect, after the restoration of one's damaged retina and the infusion of the long-lost code into our newly created consciousness as children of light, if it is only then that we can *see* this "... invisible nature, namely, his eternal power and deity, ..." then it is our place to do so. According to Paul, "what can be known about God is plain ..." in creation, even if we as a species have to be restructured internally before we can perceive it. Perhaps the Christian community, which lays claim to being this new creation in the midst of the unregenerate slime mold of secular society, should take more seriously—no, more exuberantly—its role as decipherers of the code of creation. For, also according to the Apostle, it will spell, ultimately, love: the wonder of being, of cosmos brought out of chaos.

Anthood or Anarchy?

It is strange, the sorts of images that offend us at various times in our history. During some periods we are enamoured by images of atomies, small discrete bodies of matter. Democritus, the Greek philosopher, can be credited with our first recorded description of the world in this way: a rain of falling bits of matter. This at a time when individualism was a cherished political value in his part of the world. At other points in our history, however, this image has repelled us. It is too disconnected, too fragmented, not cozily social enough for us. So we devise, in the mirrors of natural science and politics, other pictures to counteract our fear of separation and loneliness. At such times we come up with images of unity. It is then we get holism in science and socialism in politics. The interworkings of the total organism become what is most important to us. But after a while we begin to grow uneasy with our associations. Repugnance at the anthill view of man sets in, and we ricochet back again toward atomistic theories.

That quality that F. Scott Fitzgerald found so important for an artist—holding two opposing ideas balanced delicately in the mind at one time, in a word, paradox—seems as yet beyond our clumsy means, at least corporately. We stagger, unbalanced, veering first in one direction, then another. And no one seems to notice the bald-faced fact that it is only the spiritual organelles of humanity who have ever seen the need for or attained any finesse at maintaining paradox. All pragmatic parts of the organism are bent on wiping out paradox. Thus we go on, continually seesawing between particularity and unity and getting ever dizzier and dizzier in the process.

For example, the stock in holism is up at present, both in science and religion. We speak reverently of holistic man and holistic society, and much of the tremor in our voices is due to the reverberations of "holy" hinted at in the word. It is a term, however, invented in 1926 and used by entomologists to describe certain dense insect societies, multicreatured organisms such as anthills and termite nests and beehives. We shudder at the comparison of human society to an anthill, yet we feel one of those heady inhalations of ennoblement when we attach the word "holistic" to anything human.

Summer is the time for observing holism at its height. It is then that the dormant hills and nests and hives of insects bestir themselves to life again and are once more open for business. Building contracts are let for new subdivisions; the aphids are carried out to pasture on young bean and peach and rose leaves; the hatching young are fed and groomed; new sources of food are sought out. And all this work of ant civilization is managed, strange to tell, *with no apparent leadership.* The queen is only a figurehead; she is, indeed, the mother of her people, but one with no political ambitions. Nor is there a prime minister at her elbow who does the real ruling. And yet the phenomenal accomplishments of the ant, termite, and bee societies go on, seemingly by means of a corporate intelligence of which each individual is a mere unit of meaning. They meet, pass, touch antennae, bumble on, until two happen to cross paths, like neural bits, whose information forms a link which then attracts to it other neural bits finally forming a whole sentence of ant intelligence: "Dead spider to the north under the lilac bush; follow me." They are at once both the telegraph wire and the message. Cooperation is not a question. There is no persuading, no cajoling, no coercion. This is, indeed, democracy at work.

In such a well-oiled society, it should not surprise us that there are plenty of hangers-on. An entire catalogue of mites, beetles, and caterpillars manage to finagle their way into the life of the hill. At present, a total of three thousand different creatures have been documented as inhabiting this well-run hostel as guests of the establishment. Some provide minor housekeeping services, clearing away the crumbs too small even for an ant's notice. Others are out-and-out mendicants, such as a certain species of gnat that hovers

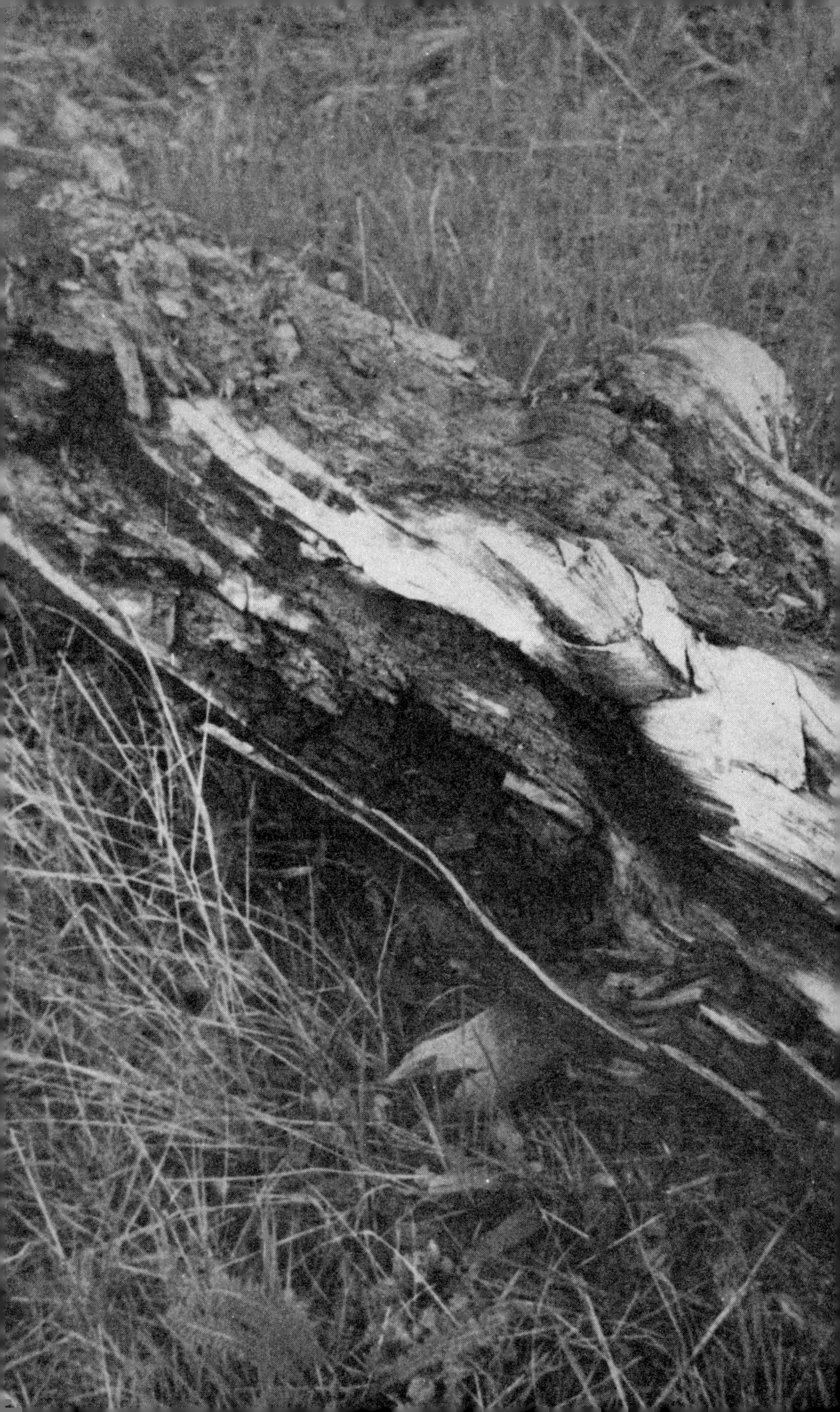

above ant trails, finally alighting to beg by the wayside until one of his more industrious cousins pauses in his busy tracks to mouth over some alms.

To carry the parallel even more uncomfortably close to home, there are even alcoholic ants who become addicted to the excretions of honey caterpillars, the kind that later emerge into blue butterflies. Although the drops of honeydew are not food for the ant, he will go to the trouble of carrying the cumbersome caterpillar back to the hill where it settles down to devour as many ant larvae as it can hold during this stage of its insect life. The worker ants that visit the honey caterpillar seem to become obsessed with the sweet liquid it secretes, and their attention to their young charges in the ant nursery, which in other situations they would die to defend, falls off miserably.

Termites, too, have a type of beetle larva living in their nests in Guyana which gives out sweet substances from abdominal glands and which the termites will drunkenly continue licking even as the beetle larva is in the act of devouring termite young. Yet these dense, holistic societies are clearly strong enough to absorb this shock to their nervous systems. There is not even an attempt made to punish or reform the addicts; presumably their fellow workers merely shrug and go on about their collective business, bearing no rancour or resentment toward the aberrationists.

Surely we should be pleased by any favorable comparison between ourselves and the ants. Practically every political goal of this century is embodied there in the hill in shining apotheosis. Even sex— which the futurists assure us is in the process of passing from the scene in a last gasping frenzy, after which we will no longer be enslaved to passion, pregnancy, or equal opportunity acts—even sex has been put in its proper, specialized place, the egg-producing queen. Minor aberrations of individuals can be dealt with and do not threaten the security of the superorganism. Is this not what we say, even swear, we want? Here is holism at its height.

Yet I know of not one human who would willingly enter the anthill. We draw back; our very flesh recoils as the antennae advance towards us, ready to receive whatever bits of data we have that will link us into the collective consciousness of the whole. Our fear of the loss of the self is overmastering. We have an immediate allergic reaction, swelling up to extend the borders of our personal space.

And we are not alone in this. All living creatures have some sort of immunological system by which they react to "foreign" bodies. Otherwise all life would have long ago become one flowing, ropy, liquid mass—something suspiciously similar to Emerson's vaporous Oversoul. In fact, however, at the first sign of encroachment upon its boundaries by another "self," the skin of a cell, coated with antigens that act as chemical antennae, sets off the alarm that produces substances called, fittingly enough, antibodies. These rush out to surround and reject the imposter. Indeed, ants themselves operate as single cells here. They all share characteristic smells derived from passing their food from mouth to mouth. Outsiders, even ants from other hills, are thus recognized as not being their fraternal messmates.

These allergic reactions are what makes the transplant business so tricky. We are, indeed, such unique organisms that our cells sniff out intruders to our bodies no matter how good their intentions. They do not recognize the validity of donor cards. Only the cells of identical twins seem to stick together spontaneously, catching the scent of a long-lost compatriot. Here is the whole direction of disease in fact: first the invasion, usually innocent enough, by foreign cells, most often bacteria or viruses; then the sensing and reaction, usually overreaction, to them.

Indeed, the cure can be worse than the disease itself, as Lewis Thomas, the president of the Memorial Sloan-Kettering Cancer Center, points out in *The Lives of a Cell.*

> Pathogenicity may be something of a disadvantage for most microbes, carrying lethal risks more frightening to them than to us. The man who catches a meningococcus is in considerably less danger for his life, even without chemotherapy, than meningococci with the bad luck to catch a man. . . . We are likely to turn on every defense at our disposal; we will bomb, defoliate, blockade, seal off, and destroy all the tissues in the area . . ., occluding capillaries and shutting off the blood supply. . . . Pyrogen is released from leukocytes, adding fever to hemorrhage, necrosis, and shock. It is a shambles.

Such is our innate autonomic cellular hypersensitivity to selfhood. We're awfully touchy about our boundaries. No wonder we are ready to settle for anarchy rather than anthood.

Nevertheless, before we reject out-of-hand the prospect of ourselves as functioning smoothly and continuously as certain insect societies do, let us recall the apostolic analogy of ourselves as members of the body of Christ. "For just as the body is one and has many members, and all the members of the body, though many, are one body, so it is with Christ." Here again, in another more acceptably human mode, is the undeniable image of the superorganism, is it not? Are we not all exhorted to contribute, interchange, suffer, and rejoice together? And has not this very analogy been the lodestone of the church for centuries? Do we not feel that this is the most exalted of human destinies, to be melded, as marriage knits the flesh of two, into this universal distance- and time-defying Body?

What makes the difference, then? Why do we call the anthill an ignoble analogy and the Body of Christ a transcendent one, one that lifts us above our present humanity which we would defend, even in its unredeemed state, against the ants?

We call the ants mindless, and so they are, except as they make up one corporate brain of which they are the extensions. And though they scurry about in their jerky, graceless fashion, doing their duty till they die, they have no consciousness of themselves as members nor can they conceptualize the hill as a whole. In fact, if they are separated from the hill, cut off from its corporate life, though well provisioned in every other way, they will die.

It is in the church that we know ourselves in both modes, as individual selves and as members of the whole, participants in a cosmic intertwining dance of creation.

It is as though every cell in one's body suddenly became conscious of its self and of its participation in the larger, more magnificent matrix of the body. Would that not simultaneously produce glorification and humility? Would not the life of such a body be enhanced to a transcendent degree by such awareness of selfhood on the part of its minutest member? Would it not be incandescent with consciousness?

It is for such expanded consciousness that we were made. Not a small, truncated selfhood staking out a niggling claim against all of creation. Nor yet an unwitting anthood, scrabbling in and out of the hill. But revealed as children of God, bearing his image in our individual selves, an image that partakes of that divine reciprocity by which life is made abundant.

The promise does not end with ourselves, however. In fact, there never seems to be an end to God's creativity. For when we become truly this transcendent Body of Christ, all creation, subjected to futility and decay, will be raised with us to fuller life. The trees will clap their hands; the hills will leap in praise; the morning star will sing, and even the ants will rejoice.

Mayflies in Gehenna

I have sat on summer lakes that hang high between mountain peaks and waited patiently for the rising of trout. There is a small liquid blip as he breaks the molten gray green membrane of the water. You turn your head sharply, seldom quick enough to catch him at it, but only in time to see the ring on the surface spreading and already disappearing.

I am no fisherman myself, but I like their company on the lake because one is necessarily absolved of all conversation except for an occasional pointed finger or a sudden intake of breath. The fisherman serves as a mooring to keep me from floating off into some stark-staring daydream when my senses creep out on business of their own and leave me, still respiring but unobservant, all alone.

On such summer lakes one often sees fragile miniature sailboats, the sterns pointing curiously upwards, reminiscent somehow of oriental outriggers. If you can scoop one from the water's surface, you will find that it is the crystallized ghost of some creature whose senses have indeed succeeded in creeping out of it altogether, leaving behind this mere shadow of its former self. What you have in your hand will doubtless be the shed exoskeleton, made of translucent chitin, belonging to a mayfly, the only insect known to molt as an adult. And it may well be that its present self, soft and struggling, is what the trout has just swallowed.

Let us turn over the lovely mayflies in our minds, another summer phenomenon that, though they do not sting and, for all their similarity to sailboats, are in their own way as offensive as ants.

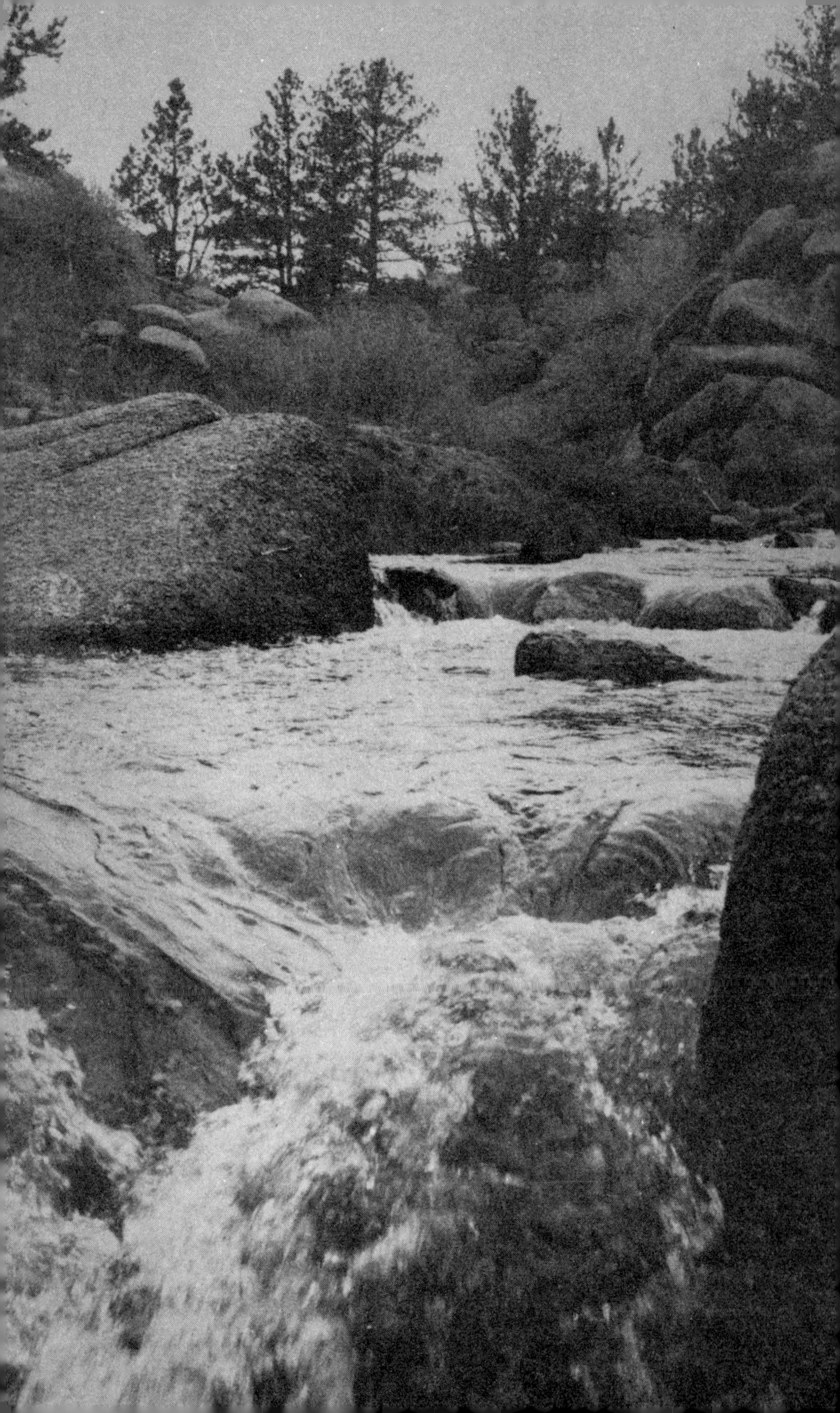

Mayflies are not civilized in the sense that ants or bees are. Their societies are much less specialized. Each takes care of his own feeding. Everyone gets to mate. They build no structures other than their own skeletons. They burrow individually into the mud of lake bottoms. Their adult lives are, indeed, too short for any kind of sophisticated antlike society. After a couple of years on the bottom of a lake bed, during which they go through thirty successive changes of clothes by shedding their nymphal skins, they finally, one fine day, rise to the top of the lake water, buoyed up by the air accumulating beneath their last aquatic shell. As each mayfly splits along the back, a new creature emerges, no longer a mud-burrower but a winged, gleaming sliver of ephemera which will never again do anything so mundane as eat.

Thus far, the mayfly's story is a pretty one. It pleases us with its theme of upward mobility. At this point we have before us the picture of the adult mayfly, a fragile, gauzy creature of fairy tales. It takes us aback to realize that it has survived all sorts of upheavals and trepidations on this orb. A companion of dinosaurs and glaciers, it has prevailed past these giants. The American naturalist Edwin Way Teale has called the mayfly one of the great paradoxes of nature: the endurance of the weak.

All this makes the mayfly even more admirable. We seem constitutionally devoted to the underdog in a story. If a mayfly can beat out a dinosaur over the long haul, we are willing to cheer her on. Yet when we discover the means used by the mayfly to maintain its line, we cannot help drawing back in disgust. For these insects survive by weight of sheer incalculable numbers. Along the shores of Lake Erie in early summer they rise like smoke. Natives call it a "mayfly storm," so severe is their encroachment on the environment.

They pile up in windrows three feet deep along the waterline. Street sweepers are almost overcome by clearing away the debris of this blizzard so that traffic can move. Often bridges are closed because of the overpasses made oil slick by crushed mayfly corpses. People shovel them into bushel baskets for garden fertilizer. Their smell, like decaying fish, pervades the atmosphere. All buildings, fences, telephone poles are furred with their clinging forms. The folds of one's clothes are filled with them. Outdoor lighting has to be turned off for the duration. Ferries to the lake islands must ply back and forth in all but total darkness. These creatures that individually seem weightless cause the trees, the weeds, the power lines to sag beneath their overwhelming numbers.

The delicate beauty of a single mayfly becomes a grotesquerie when multiplied by millions. Just as a sturdy Anglo-Saxon word that has served us faithfully all our literate lives can metamorphose into a mocking horror of nonsense if repeated a dozen, a hundred times in succession, so the mayfly, beautiful, fragile, and cunningly wrought in its single self, changes to a repellent, clinging monster through the sheer force of repetition. Our sense of proportion is mortally wounded. Prodigality in nature is a problem we cannot fathom. Indeed, we hardly dare approach it for fear.

From the human point of view, the waste involved in maintaining life on this planet is enormous. The universe is not cost-efficient. The mayflies that manage to mate in their great orgasmic marriage clouds produce 1,500 eggs each, most of which go to supply provender for other aquatic life. Those that succeed in making it to larvahood are similarly endangered by hungry lake dwellers. Should they shed the requisite thirty hides that lead to maturity, most are even then picked off by birds, squelched under automobile tires, washed down by hoses, captured by gray ground spiders. Frankly, the chances for a mayfly's fulfillment in life are slim.

We may be willing to grant, though grudgingly, the utility of the numbers that go to supply fodder for other species. Those have at least, however unwittingly, filled a purpose, though why a life cycle so complex should be thus rudely interrupted in mid-course is hard to understand. But the ones that die ignominiously smeared across the windshield—this is waste of the most unconscionable sort.

The laws of thermodynamics, so elegantly poised upon the point of the fulcrum, not allowing a single photon to fall away into nothingness, have no counterpart, it seems, in the economy of life forms. Here the rule is prodigality. A lavish laying on of life only to be wiped away with a dirty rag.

If economy is the law of light, waste seems the general tendency of life. Unfulfillment is the rule rather than the exception. And in this case, it is nature who holds the mirror up to us rather than the other way around. The image we see in the natural world we take, naturally enough, for a paradigm of our own condition. We are terrorized at the thought of dying, like flies, in multitudes. The waste overwhelms us. Will our flesh, too, finally be made negligible by numbers? Do we live only to be used as fertilizer for some untended garden?

We are continually cautioned against wasting our time, wasting our money, wasting our opportunities. Yet what other example has been set us? Everywhere we look—the more life, the more waste. We take it for granted that cultures teeming with the burden of superfluous bodies hold human life cheap. Numbers have that effect on us.

At this point there is a pause and a deep breath in the argument. Already we have begun to marshal our apologetics and Scripture references to counteract this seeming slur upon the character of the Creator. But before we appeal to the hairs of our head or point to the sparrows falling out of the sky as evidence of the intimate attention paid by the Craftsman to his handiwork, let us remember that hell, when it does not mean simply Sheol or Hades, the place of the dead, means instead Gehenna, the garbage dump, the refuse heap. It must be filled to near bursting by now with all sorts of life not brought to completion. Mayflies and dinosaurs and humans alike have it bulging at the seams, no doubt. For I wouldn't want to put our statistics as a species up against even those of mayflies. The number of people I come across, bent on fulfilling their destiny, of cracking open their larval skins time after time, of growing into the full stature of Christ, is miniscule. Taken as a category of creation, we are most often content to burrow into the mud at the lake bottom.

How much choice we have about this remains an open question. Being products of Western civilization and only grafted-in shoots on what is essentially an Eastern religion, we tend to place a great deal more emphasis on individual effort than we find in the original stock. The parable of the sower, if read with strict attention to the text, is bound to make the sons of Dale Carnegie uneasy. Some of the seed, it seems, was doomed from the start. It found itself in the same existential position as a mayfly larva swallowed by a browsing carp or a Biafran beggar-child whose protein molecules will never make the right connections.

It is not just nature in its profligacy that offends us. So does the gospel. Jesus, in his parables, is never sentimental about the processes of nature. We are wont to linger over the lilies of the field in their prime while he goes on to describe their decline: "'. . . which today is alive and tomorrow is thrown into the oven. . . .'" Our sense of fairness is outraged by the sower's superfluous seeds and the smoldering lilies. Waste is not right. We have the laws of thermodynamics and Benjamin Franklin to prove it. The dump is not our proper end.

The only counterpoise I have to that most moral and undeniably just claim is the cross. Planted firmly in the garbage heap that was at once Golgotha and Gehenna, the Lily of the Valley himself is cast into the oven. It must be a heavy weight, indeed, that can balance the waste of the world. We can raise our fists to heaven and rail against the unfair economy of creation. But meanwhile the Creator himself hangs, dying for man and mayfly, by some as yet dimly featured law of his own making, salvaging from futility the wasted multitudes.

The Separate Reality

Late in the afternoon I often go out walking with my dog in the hills around my home. Such excursions have the character of escape. I climb over a sagging, barbed-wire fence and am free. This twisted metal thread, gradually being engulfed by wild red currant bushes that birds have planted while swinging on the wire, separates one reality from another. My dog and I both sense this.

We follow the natural divisions of the land as we walk—a rock fault, the crest of a hill, a dry creek bed. It takes only a few minutes for the authority of this other reality to make itself felt. In this sphere one must be silent and stare. There are no interposing "media." There is no "sharing."

I stare at a white-skinned, black-scarred aspen tree whose autumnal leaves have turned a rosy gold with the trapped anthocyanin left by the receding sap. The tree and I do not communicate. Yet as I rub my hand across its tough skin and scabs and feel my own sap, full of sugars and enzymes, circulating through the branches of my body, I once again sustain the momentary illusion that, given such a setting of steady, silent intent, of beauty, I would find it easy and natural to be good and virtuous forever. Here every organism goes about its business with unwearying devotion. Sap rising and falling. Leaves drifting and decaying. Birds eating and excreting. Seeds dying and sprouting. Surely I could slip into a niche somewhere in this open-air monastery.

I sit down under the tree and call my dog to me. He is a comical sight, sniffing his way over the hill in systematic crisscrosses of ecstasy, belonging yet not belonging to this separate reality. Watching him, I realize that his devotion to his destiny is greater than mine. With a few exceptions, mostly in the form of squirrels, he is obedient, faithful, and affectionate toward his master. In that great avalanche of creation we call the fall he has landed somewhere between me and the tree. He is that strange anomaly, a domesticated animal.

This separate reality my dog and I invade was invented in the eighteenth century, and it is called Nature. It contains the images that float before our mind's eye when we hear the word "Creation": trees and birds and flowers and fish. Ruffed grouse and black bears, gray whales and mule deer. It is the preferred setting for Boy Scout jamborees, rock concerts, vacations, and summer weddings. We reverently preserve this separate reality called nature in national parks and game sanctuaries.

But we do not allow it in the house. It is useless to point out that gravity operates indoors as well as out, that bacteria decompose garbage in the trash can, that water evaporates from the sink. Those activities of the physical world, while acknowledged as Science, are outside our common category of Nature. The closest we come to Nature indoors is pine-scented room deodorizer.

Yet Nature, or at any rate Creation, has always been a significant category in Christian understanding. Significant but not static. For example, the comparable category for the first-century Greek world was the cosmos. The Greek cosmos differs from our Nature in that it contains all things that have being, including mathematics and time. Only cursory attention is given to small furry animals and fields of daisies. Thus there arose in the first few hundred years of the church life-and-death controversies over the "nature" of Christ: how he came into being; what that being, in an almost mathematical and molecular sense, consists of; how it relates to temporal history. These concerns, imbedded in the Nicene Creed, now seem almost inaccessibly antiquarian to the contemporary Christian. "Very God of Very God; Begotten, not made; Being of one substance with the Father." That was the closest approximation to a "nature talk" the early church in its Greek milieu ever made.

It remained for Tennyson, a milennium and a half later, to translate that cosmological obsession into our familiar Nature terms:

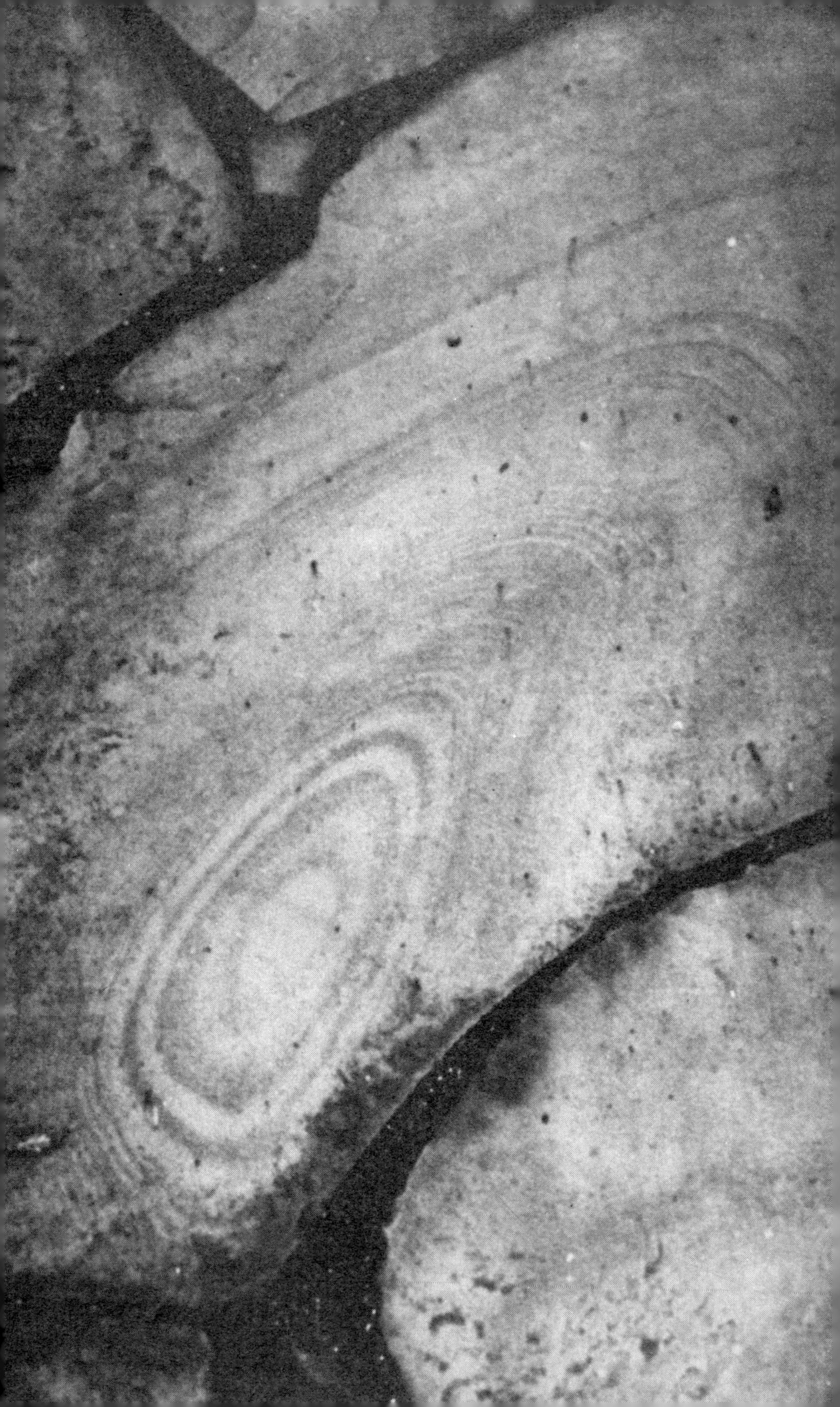

> Flower in the crannied wall,
> I pluck you out of the crannies;
> I hold you here, root and all, in my hand,
> Little flower—but *if* I could understand
> What you are, root and all, and all in all,
> I should know what God and man is.

Well, we may say, we will leapfrog over the esoteric Greeks and get back to those earthy Hebrews. *They* understood about Nature. Didn't Jacob camp out with a rock for a pillow? And Moses, out on a nature walk, discovered a new and truly wild flower, a burning bush. But that's not exactly what we had in mind either. That's a good deal more than we ask of Nature today. Indeed, we won't put up with its getting so out of hand. It is the steady predictability of Nature we love—the rotating seasons, the weather forecast, the ecological balance.

But for the Hebrews, the category we call Nature, one for which they had no word at all, was always precarious and unpredictable, capable of breaking forth into flame or dropping bread down on their heads or washing away the world in a few weeks. Jacob's pillow became the first step on the stairway to heaven. Anything one touched, any place one innocently laid one's head, could be an unlooked-for entrance into the unveiled presence of the Creator. Trees and rocks and streams were alive with the possibilities of what God might decide to do next. And although the Old Testament escapes the sentimentality of latter-day pantheism, the prospects of Yahweh's showing up in a whirlwind or a thunderclap were enough to encourage the Hebrews to keep a wary eye on the environment.

They also insisted upon its joining the chorus of praise to its Creator. The psalmist orders the trees to clap their hands and the hills to leap for joy. We even have it on no less a Hebrew authority than Jesus that the very stones could cry out in praise of the King of heaven, in addition to performing the formidable task of raising up children to Abraham.

Yes, Nature has suffered a considerable comedown since the days of the "earthy" Hebrews. We tend to place the burden of this responsibility on the thin shoulders of Sir Isaac Newton, who in the eighteenth century formulated the binomial theorem, the laws of gravity and motion, and the elements of differential calculus. The poets who inherited this vivisection of the world were particularly distressed with Newton's study of light. Blake, for example, scorned both the Greek's cosmology and Newton's science, preferring to cast his lot with the Hebrews, when he wrote:

> The Atoms of Democritus
> And Newton's Particles of Light
> Are sands upon the Red Sea shore,
> Where Israel's tents do shine so bright.

But such a dividing of waters of creation into Nature and Science must have begun even earlier in the church's history. On one side of the gulf we see the Scholastics, for whom Nature was primarily a proposition in an interminable argument that was to prove the existence of God. On the other side stands Francis of Assisi, birds perched in his hair, proclaiming his kinship with the sun and moon. Give them a few centuries, and the Scholastics in their cold, stone edifices of the University of Paris have become Isaac Newton at Cambridge writing his *Philosophiae Naturalis Principia Mathematica* in which Nature becomes Number. Now Newton was a pious man who also wrote treatises on Daniel and Revelation. To him the numbers added up to God. But to his followers they added up only to Science.

And what of the inheritors of Saint Francis? As the eighteenth century turned into the nineteenth, they either went mad like Blake, died early and unresolved like Shelley and Keats, or lived to a ripe old age writing silly things about the "natural piety" of the pagan like Wordsworth. Ironically, it was the mad Blake who could recognize nonsense: "I see in Wordsworth the Natural Man rising up against the Spiritual Man Continually, & then he is No Poet but a Heathen Philosopher at Enmity against all true Poetry or Inspiration. There is no such Thing as Natural Piety Because The Natural Man is at Enmity with God."

Yet when Wordsworth wrote his famous sonnet celebrating that pious pagan, "suckled in a creed outworn," it was the first three lines that became the motto for that wistful, slightly comical creature, the twentieth-century nature lover.

> The world is too much with us; late and soon,
> Getting and spending, we lay waste our powers:
> Little we see in Nature that is ours. . . .

At last. There is the use of the term "Nature" we have been looking for. There are the wandering clouds and fields of daffodils and the babbling brooks. And there, too, is the divorce of Nature from "the world" that is also a part of our understanding. Human beings and their society forever separated from Nature. Henceforth, we can only be picnickers or backpackers, inserting ourselves as unobtrusively as possible into the landscape, scrupulously gathering up our sandwich bags and virtuously picking up the aluminum cans others have left behind. We refrain from picking the wild flowers and shoot wild animals only with a camera. But at last we must go home and sadly shut the door on Nature.

True, for its part Nature will not have us on any account. At a recent national campers' convention a few miles from my home, the very grass disintegrated within two days under the hiking boots of pious pagans. The game removed themselves to the next county. Pollen grains and mosquitoes filled the air. The campers were humble toward the mosquitoes and apologetic about the grass. Still, Nature has a way of receding upon our approach, like one who is not anxious to make friends.

Yet we persist, pagans and Christians alike. "Take us back," we whimper, plucking at the sleeve of heartless Mother Nature. We may not, as a culture, have penetrated to the meaning of disobedience in the Garden, but we have certainly appropriated the fact of expulsion from it. We stand somewhat bewildered beyond the gates, wondering why the sight of a scurrying furry animal should move us so when we don't even remember its name.

The greater this gulf between Nature and the world, the easier it becomes to delude ourselves about our invulnerability. We may lament Nature's elusiveness, but we also feel safe from its surprises. That is why termites in the woodwork and cancer in the bloodstream always come as a shock. Despite the "unnaturalness" of fallen humanity, Nature has been allowed to keep a grip on our bodies, our breath, our bacteria.

How far we have withdrawn into our illusory citadel can be

measured by our distance from the Franciscan hymn that begins, sweetly enough, "Praised be God for our Sister, Mother Earth, which brings forth varied fruits and grass and glowing flowers," but ends on the shocking note, "Praised be God for our Sister, the death of the body." That is truly a nature psalm, embracing all the mysterious implications of our kinship with creation.

Indeed, it would be a great boon to all human culture if Christianity could succeed in once more uniting Nature and Number. We have heard for long yawning decades now about the war between science and religion and their imminent reconciliation at the hands of Christian apologists. These announcements would be much more credible if they came from Christian scientists. In the twentieth century, Christendom has embraced Nature more passionately than our forebears ever did. Lilies of the field leave us positively giddy. But too close an embrace makes respectful attention impossible. Our love is more often a consumer's orgy. We must possess Nature. We protect the lilies and feed the sparrows, hoping to make them ours.

Stand back a bit, and instead of "loving" nature, do as Jesus instructed and consider it. Observe where the constellation Scorpio rises in the summer sky. Learn how long light takes to reach the earth from our own sister sun and why it is at present impossible to calculate accurately either the distance or size of strange quasars. Follow the seedpods of field flowers and the hundred curious paths by which they find their way into the ground. Discover what cancer cells look like. Jonathan Edwards knew, much more intimately than Tennyson, the anatomy of arachnids. The one is content to stand with his uprooted flower drooping like a dismal question mark in his disappointed hand, while the other pursues spiders to his satisfaction.

This is the only significance of the science-and-religion reconciliation, not that scores of doubting scientists will be converted, but that thousands of blurry-eyed, nature-loving Christians will shake themselves, blink, and begin to take a hard, intimate, respectful look at the handiwork of their Creator. That they will sit down silently on a stump or a rock somewhere and feel the listening, watching, thrumming sense of separation and groaning desire that engulfs them—the separation that makes it painfully impossible for human beings to live like lilies and the desire that makes it equally impossible to stop trying.

Yet even in the continual tension we must suffer between these separate realities of "the world" and Nature, there is a grace extended to us, often misappropriated but nevertheless real. It is the very quality of carelessness, of what-will-it-matter-fifty-years-from-now. It is freedom from self-importance and egotism that dissipates in the open air like smoke. Misappropriated and turned inside out, it is the frequently described fear that assails the solitary figure overwhelmed by the night sky, filled as it is with vast spaces and infinite stars. But it is that very sense of not mattering that comforts the heart of Sam the hobbit, struggling with the outsized task of saving Tolkien's Middle-earth. Within the very realm of the Enemy, he has a moment of carelessness mediated by the sight of a star.

> There, peeping among the cloud-wrack above a dark tor high up in the mountains, Sam saw a white star twinkle for a while. The beauty of it smote his heart, as he looked up out of the forsaken land, and hope returned to him. For like a shaft, clear and cold, the thought pierced him that in the end the Shadow was only a small and passing thing; there was light and high beauty for ever beyond its reach. . . . Now, for a moment, his own fate, and even his master's, ceased to trouble him.

Notice that Sam did not, like Dorothy in the Land of Oz, begin to sing about wishing on a star. He did not attempt to "commune" with Nature in the shape of a star. He recognized it as a separate—but substantial—reality. Far from frightening him, the thought of his own inconsequence comforted him. Field flowers being burnt in the oven, numbered sparrows falling out of the sky, seeds buried in the earth. It is by such strange paradoxes that Nature talks to us.

"Ripeness Is All"

My garden dies early. At 7,000 feet, though there may be a long, luxurious Indian summer following the first frost, the tomato plants and bean vines hang, blackened and stiff on their stakes, like a vegetable *memento mori*. They are such an affront, aesthetically and cosmically, that as soon as the weather warms again I rip their roots from the damp, clinging soil and make great heaps of tomato, bean, squash, and cucumber carcasses with a strange, purging sense of vengeance. No matter how abundantly they have borne, I feel somehow they have betrayed me. I have never been one to romanticize the barren fig tree. I lie in bed on that first cold night, grinding my teeth while I imagine I can hear the cells splitting their sides as their liquid life freezes and swells.

Of course, the underground tribe go on smugly sleeping and fattening through it all. I don't even bother to dig up my carrots and onions until late October, after which they are not likely to be discoverable beneath the snow. Perhaps because of their patient perseverance, roots are always the lowliest, most humble of our foods. Potatoes, turnips, beets. Poor folks' fare all over the world.

So after the first frost and before the heavy snows, I go out to prepare the garden for winter. I heap up the dead vines, layer them with damp dirt to speed the decaying process, loosen the soil around the root tribe so they can be easily pulled and stored, and finally turn the whole plot over, shovelful by shovelful, so that the winter will fill the ground with moisture and tenderize the tough earth by its repeated freezing and thawing. It is the end of the cycle. My last duty to this patch of the world where I have labored all summer. All I will be able to do from now on is to pull the curtain back on cold days and stare at the raw wound through the frozen months, enduring the process that is the dark underside of fertility.

As I sink the shovel into the resilient earth, I remember, even if only with my foot as it feels the ground give beneath the blade, that I am reenacting that primordial rite to which we still have access only by a now almost indistinguishable path. For if the Messiah came today and to our country, it would be impossible for him to wander about the countryside, go off to the hills to pray, sit on a slope and teach from the realities of seed and field and harvest. Oh, maybe in our little village, which numbers fewer than two hundred souls, he could gather a small crowd in Leland Counze's field on the other side of the creek. But not one of five thousand. Farmers have learned to be wary of anything remotely resembling a rock concert, as no doubt the Gadarene swineherd learned to suspect the cost of exorcism.

But by and large our society no longer learns from organic metaphors. Our images are machines that do not grow but only accrete. (Nor, unfortunately, when they die, do they fall into the ground and disintegrate.) I turn over another black lump of dirt and watch a mauve and terra-cotta earthworm wriggle away, confused by the disruption of his home. "The kingdom of heaven is like. . . ." *Is there some correlation lacking here?* I wonder as I pick out the stones my shovel has struck against and cast them further down the hillside. Can we know what the kingdom of heaven is like when we no longer experience the metaphors that manifested it? If we've never harvested a crop or fished, do we miss something essential about the great ingathering of souls? Do bureaucratic "models for ministry" really supplant the whole truth of sheep feeding and grain reaping?

There is a correspondence between creation and the kingdom that will not be denied. Nothing of our own manufacture proves sufficient to carry that freight of meaning. This is why attention to creation is more than a pleasant exercise. "I do not see how the 'fear' of God could have ever meant to me anything but the lowest prudential efforts to be safe," says C. S. Lewis, "if I had never seen certain ominous ravines and unapproachable crags." And we have the witness of at least one thoughtful pagan, Thoreau, that "the very globe continually transcends and translates itself. . . . Even ice

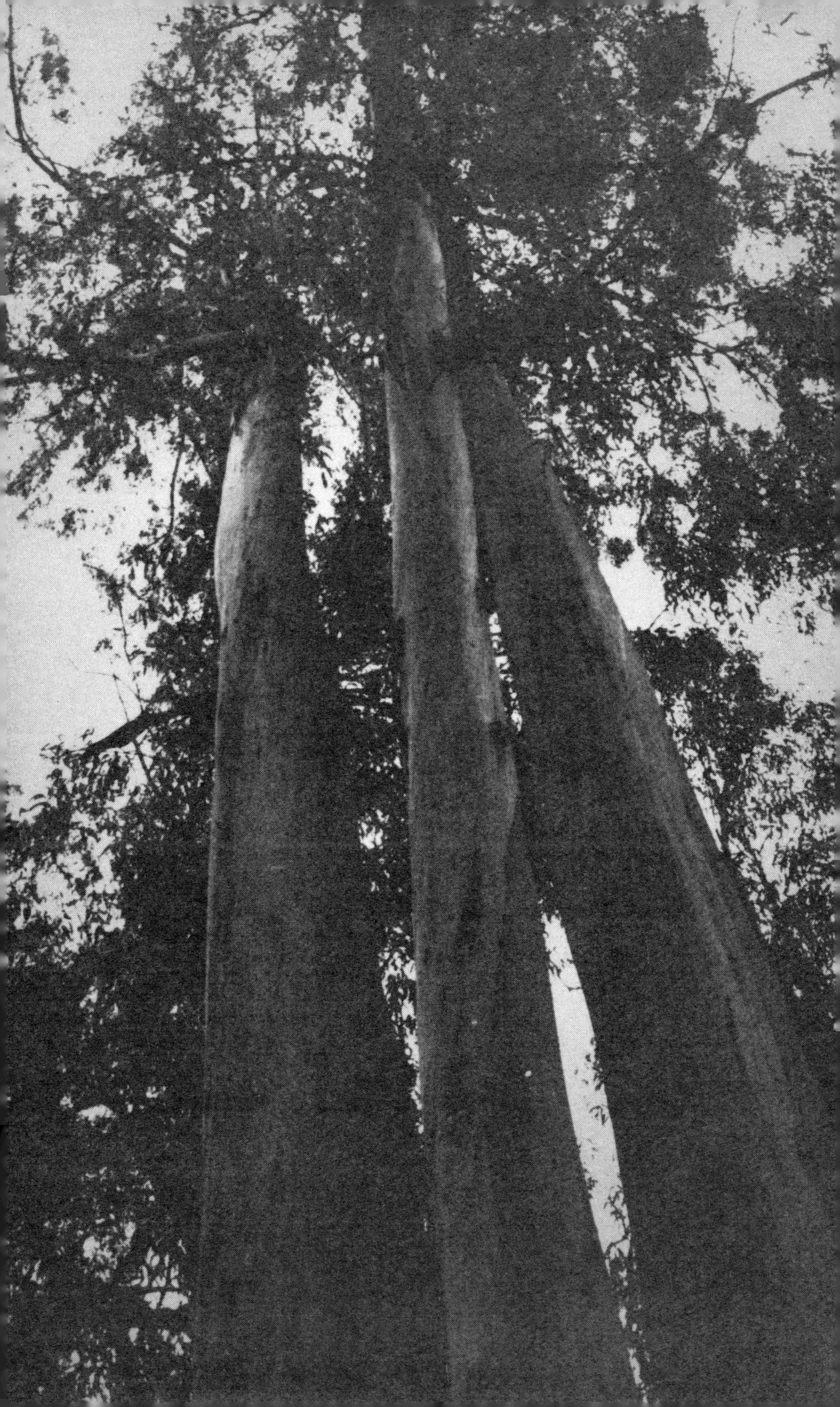

begins with delicate crystal leaves, as if it had flowed into moulds which the fronds of water plants have impressed on the watery mirror. The whole tree itself is but one leaf, and rivers are still vaster leaves whose pulp is intervening earth. . . ." The shapes we find under an electron microscope are repeated in the macrocosm all about us. Magnitude mirrors the miniscule. The visible echoes the invisible. To call Jesus the Light of the world is no mere expression of sentiment. It acknowledges our phototropism on all levels of being; all that glitters, gold or not, we are drawn to. A president may wear a pin-striped suit, but a king must shine and be resplendent.

    I have heard religious leaders attempt to shrug off these correspondences as mere figures of speech from which meaning is detachable. Their assumption is that analogies are interchangeable, nothing more than tools that have no reality apart from our ability to manipulate them. Little do they know of the life that lurks behind and between the lines.

    A heady scent rises from the earth in autumn. White strips of beneficent bacteria irradiate the soil with potent decay. Buried treasure. Aureomycin, I speculate. Indians used to pack wounds with a certain kind of rich, pungent earth. What I wouldn't give for several cubic yards of leaf mold from the deciduous south on this rigid western ground! I yank up a fistful of bean vines and find on the roots, true to the promise of botany classes, the little nodules of nitrogen-fixing bacteria, regular underground factories of nutrition. My vengeance against the bean vines slips away, and I can forgive them their lack of hardiness. This is like a whole new crop, this network of knots that means richness for next year.

    I set my shovel to the ground again, feel the sun slant across my shoulder, and suddenly am transported back further than the Galilean hillside and the agrarian parables. All at once I feel the root of my father Adam, dark and hidden in the earth and piled-up eons of time. What he was I am: a tiller of the soil. Bite by bite my shovel eats it, faster than the earthworm but with the same intent:

> "in toil you shall eat of it all the
>   days of your life;
> thorns and thistles it shall bring
>   forth to you;

> and you shall eat the plants of the field."

We could stand side by side, Adam and I, he in his skin shirt and I in my grubby jeans, hoeing, stopping to tear out an upstart cocklebur, pausing to lean on the hoe handle while we stare out at the horizon, wondering what weather this night will bring. We inhabit the same spiritual space. Not one moment separates us in our understanding of our place in the universe. Adam and Adam's child, cursed and blessed from the same ground.

Perhaps that is what is at the root of the widely touted therapy of gardening: the recognition of one's human contingency. In a culture where that fact is disguised or ignored as often as possible, where climate is controlled, livings made inside buildings, foods processed beyond recognition, there is very little evidence of our ancestral link to Adam. We build machines to do our planting and harvesting or, where that is not yet feasible, hire others to produce the "sweat of the face" whereby we shall eat our bread. For there is really no reason for gardening other than keeping this cord alive to our past, our origin. Economically it makes no sense at all. One can buy, bug free and cellophane wrapped, all the garden produce one needs at the supermarket and at a much lower price if one considers time as money. Why then do we feel that surge of ecstasy when we see the saffron treasure of carrots laid out on the black dirt like coins on velvet? Is it because the economy of the contemporary marketplace is not the economy of the kingdom of heaven or even of our human ancestry? Time is more than currency.

The garden is the place where we can, if only at infrequent intervals, escape from the land of Nod—the land of Wandering, as some translate it—the land of rootlessness where we are cut off from our patrimony and where the ground "shall no longer yield to you its strength." In the garden we are at home as humans. Not as in that first home, the first Garden that lies forever closed to us, but at least close enough to feel our great progenitor beside us, and with him the whole of humanity—all those legions who have bent their backs over a hoe, all those millions whom we currently insulate ourselves from, whose eyes still search the sky for signs of rain. The garden is perhaps the place of our most efficacious spiritual therapy. Or to paraphrase

Thomas Merton, who can be neurotic in front of a carrot?

The rattling cornstalks on the west edge of my garden come down last. They die with a little more dignity; instead of simply going slack and bruised, they gradually turn a pale umber, their tassels the color of ripe wheat. The dry rattle of the wind moving through their lancelike leaves keeps me company while I bury the bodies of their less-sturdy companions in compost heaps. But finally they, too, must come down, or the snow will turn them black and moldy, and their disgraceful standing death will reproach me all winter. Because of their tough, fibrous nature, the cornstalks' end is a funeral pyre.

All around me the wasps and bees collide clumsily with the moist mounds of rotting vegetation and earth. In the fall all insects die either drunk or senile. Their slow, sluggish bumbling is somehow more irritating than their sting; all their kamikaze spirit wanes with the hours of sunlight. Box-elder bugs swarm all over unlikely places. Only the indomitable earthworm, immune to light, burrows deeper just as he has done since he thawed out this spring. In what curious crook will the freeze find him this time? Perhaps he is unaware of time at all, the long months between freezing and thawing only a moment's interruption to his intraterrestrial travel.

Light. For these plant bodies I am burying, light has been their food. All summer long they have been munching away on photons, converting them into energy and growth. Their chloroplasts inhabit the plant body in almost the same way our minds inhabit us. They grow and multiply independently of the cells they live in, and when the last chloroplast has been lost or destroyed, the cell never makes any more. Its life is over.

Then the chromoplasts, subsidiaries in the work of capturing and processing photons, are allowed to show their true colors: the yellow and red of the carotenoid pigments, the anthocyanins dissolved in the cell sap—red when the sap is acid, blue when it is alkaline. These are the flags, the bright standards, of a falling army. They lie in brilliant heaps like the treasures in the tombs of kings. For a season they have eaten light; now they will be eaten themselves in the dark underground.

According to our best speculative research, the rate at which living beings die and consume each other is so high that they would be wiped from the earth's face in one human generation if there were not this process provided for the reconstituting of organic matter. In the lovely economy of light and life, the basic materials of carbon dioxide and water can be used again and again. We breathe in the exhalations of the plants, and they breathe in ours. But the energy released by rotting organic matter is simply dissipated into space as heat. That lost energy must be constantly replenished by the sun. If we were left in darkness, all our warmth would soon be given up.

I look around me. There it is. *All is safely gathered in* and the rest, from the blighted squash to the bolted lettuce, I have sent down into darkness. I stand in the middle of my digging, surrounded by death. The breathtakingly beautiful gold-leaved cottonwoods glittering against the blue dome headed toward the winter solstice— they are only the ornaments of the death ship we sail on every year. Like the jeweled treasure ship of Sutton Hoo, our earth is sailing out, out, out into the descending darkness. Its colors glow, polished by the wind. No longer greenly langorous, our blood stirs, eager for encounter with our destiny. We are leaving the light behind, having stored in our hold what we could harvest of it, something to sustain us during our planetary voyage.

All about me the earth is dying, and I smile on it benignly. A decent decay settles over the land. It is congruous; it fits all I know to be true about the world. It is not the obscene incongruity of a machine gun suddenly spitting through the midst of a flowering plum thicket, not Cain rising up against his brother Abel in sudden violence. That kind of death causes blood to cry out from the ground. This is rather the death of Abraham, ending his life old and full of years.

My garden gets me ready for death. For if I, with that shadowy Adam at my elbow, live under the same curse he did, I have leisure to contemplate the death that is coming toward me. It can come after the span of a season when my life has borne its fruit. It can come with the decent dignity I have learned from the earth. I shall not be ashamed to sift my molecules of matter into the succulent soil with the beans and corn as companions. God's curse always modulates into blessing.

But more than that. I shall myself become a voice in that great chorus of creation groaning in travail, in birth pangs, waiting through the long dark winter to be set free from decay for "the redemption of our bodies" and the springing forth of the children of God. Then my ancestor Adam shall be no longer a shadow.

Notes

Page 9

Charles Williams, *Descent of the Dove* (London: Oxford University Press, 1939), p. 58.

Page 10

Ibid., p. 57.

Page 12

Jonathan Edwards, *Original Sin,* ed. Clyde A. Holbrook (New Haven: Yale University Press, 1970), pp. 400-401.

Annie Dillard, *Pilgrim at Tinker Creek* (New York: Harper's Magazine Press, 1974), p. 266.

Page 13

Andrew Wyeth, *The Work of Andrew Wyeth* (Boston: Houghton Mifflin Company, 1968), p. 37.

Rachel Peden, *Speak to the Earth* (New York: Alfred A. Knopf, Inc., 1974), p. 82.

Page 14

Robin Lakoff, *Language and Woman's Place* (New York: Harper & Row, Publishers, Inc., 1975).

The Pulitzer Prize Plays, ed. Kathryn Coe and William H. Cordell (New York: Random House, Inc., 1935), p. 1026.

Page 15

Annie Dillard, *op. cit.,* p. 270.

Page 23

Richard Byrd, *Alone* (New York: G. P. Putnam's Sons, 1938), p. 5.

Page 24

Henry Thoreau, *Walden and "Civil Disobedience,"* ed. Owen Thomas (New York: W. W. Norton & Co., Inc., 1966), p. 186.

Byrd, *op. cit.*, p. 7.

Page 33

Ibid., p. 27.

Page 35

Corydon Bell, *The Wonder of Snow* (New York: Hill and Wang, 1957), p. 55.

Page 36

Byrd, *op. cit.*, p. 85.

Ibid., p. 109.

Page 37

Job 38:29-30.

C. S. Lewis, *Perelandra* (New York: Macmillan, Inc., 1947), pp. 183-184.

Byrd, *op. cit.*, p. 123.

Page 38

Job 39:13.

Page 39

Robert Burton, *Anatomy of Melancholy,* ed. Floyd Dell and Paul Jordan-Smith (New York: Tudor Publishing Company, 1938).

Page 44

Psalm 36:9.

Page 46

Ernst von Khuon, *The Invisible Made Visible* (Boston: New York Graphic Society Books, 1968), pp. 165-166.

Page 48

Douglas Gilbert and Clyde S. Kilby, *C. S. Lewis: Images of His World* (Grand Rapids, Mich.: Wm. B. Eerdmans Publishing Company, 1973), p. 175.

Page 49
1 Corinthians 13:12.

Page 50
Psalm 34:8.

Page 53
Isaac Asimov, *The New Intelligent Man's Guide to Science* (New York: Basic Books, Inc., Publishers, 1965), p. 318.
Ibid.

Page 54
Prince Louis de Broglie, *Matter and Light* (New York: W. W. Norton & Co., Inc., 1939), p. 37.
Ibid.
Asimov, *op. cit.,* p. 329.

Page 55
Dante, *Paradise,* Canto XXXIII, ll. 100-106, trans. Dorothy Sayers (New York: Basic Books, Inc., Publishers, 1962), p. 346.

Page 56
John 1:9.
Gilbert and Kilby, *op. cit.,* p. 166.
John 18:37, KJV.

Page 60
Romans 1:23.
Romans 1:20.

Page 63
G. K. Chesterton, *Orthodoxy* (London: John Lane, 1912), pp. 95-96.

Page 65
Romans 1:20.
Romans 1:23.

Page 70
Maurice Burton, *Just Like an Animal* (New York: Charles Scribner's Sons, 1978).
Romans 1:19-20.

Page 75

Lewis Thomas, *The Lives of a Cell* (New York: The Viking Press, 1974), pp. 77-79.

Page 76

1 Corinthians 12:12.

Page 84

Matthew 6:30.

Page 88

Complete Poetical Works of Tennyson, ed. W. J. Rolfe (Boston: Houghton Mifflin Company, 1898).

Page 89

The Poetical Works of William Blake, ed. John Sampson (London: Oxford University Press, 1956).
English Romantic Poetry and Prose, ed. Russell Noyes (New York: Oxford University Press, Inc., 1956).
The Complete Poetical Works of Wordsworth, ed. Andrew J. George (Boston: Houghton Mifflin Company, 1932).

Page 90

Ibid.

Page 91

G. K. Chesterton, *Saint Francis of Assisi* (New York: Doubleday & Co., Inc., 1924).

Page 92

J. R. R. Tolkien, *Return of the King,* rev. ed. (Boston: Houghton Mifflin Company, 1965), p. 199.

Page 94

Gilbert and Kilby, *op. cit.,* p. 166.

Page 96

Thoreau, *op. cit.,* p. 202.

Page 97

Genesis 3:17*b*-18.
Genesis 4:12.